WHY TERRARIUMS?

Terrariums flourish anywhere. They are perfect for apartments. With little time and a minimum of care, the indoor gardener can create a dust free atmosphere for his greenery. Even in the darkest of apartments a terrarium will thrive, bringing a special warm glow to winter nights.

During any season of the year you can grow cacti from Arizona, mosses native to South Carolina, ivy, orchids, begonias or pine trees. You can arrange complete terrarium gardens.

Terrariums provide the answer to the problems of the indoor gardener, but they decorate a beach house terrace or a screened-in porch as well. They are a creative experience for all plant lovers.

BARBARA JOAN GRUBMAN

INTRODUCTION TO TERRARIUMS

A STEP-BY-STEP GUIDE

ILLUSTRATIONS BY
ANN BRUCE CHAMBERLAIN

POPULAR LIBRARY ● NEW YORK

With love for Don, Lee and Matthew
the three men in my life. . .

ACKNOWLEDGMENTS

For their faith in my ability and their unflagging enthusiasm for this book, I am deeply grateful to my husband and my boys. It is they who sweated with me, rejoiced with me and understood when dinners were late, tempers short and deadlines near.

Others, too, were special helps. At the very beginning of my research, I visited A. A. Schnierow's Nursery in San Fernando, California and was greeted with warmth and kindness. Betsy Duffy allowed me to observe her while she made numerous bubble terrariums. Marcia Guzman suggested that I try my hand at them and guided me along the way. Carmen Prieto gave freely of her knowledge of plants and soil. All three helped to start this project off on a positive note and I thank them for it.

I am especially indebted to Rose Marie Reyes who typed the manuscript, thereby freeing me from a job of which I am not particularly fond. She was literally my right and my left hand!

. . . and to Kiki Roe who not only gave me support, but a quiet office in which to work, I offer my gratitude.

June, 1972

— Barbara Joan Grubman
Tarzana, California

CONTENTS

INTRODUCTION TO
TERRARIUMS
A STEP-BY-STEP GUIDE

PART I
PLANTS, TOOLS AND SUPPLIES

CHAPTER ONE:
TERRARIUMS
ENTER YOUR LIFE

Terrariums are sprouting up everywhere. They are the nowest way to display and enjoy your plants and flowers. We see them in florist shops, friends' homes and in schoolrooms. They delight the eye and call upon one's sense of design and desire to live with growing things. Whole new vistas are open to you when you decide to make one. The possibilities of these glass-encased gardens are limited only by your own imagination, so allow it to take wing and soar.

A lacy Emerald-feather fern, while delightful to look at in its terra cotta pot, becomes a thing of true beauty when it is covered with a glass dome. Its delicate leaves are even more sharply defined, as if viewed through a window, giving one the feeling of a very special glimpse of nature.

The miniature peperomia with its heart-shaped silver-striped leaves takes on a whole new dimension in a glass bubble. And the velvety loveliness of a flowering African violet will be even more pronounced when it is seen in its own small greenhouse.

Allow your thoughts to meander into the woods as you shop for your Maidenhair ferns; feel once again the warmth of the midday sun on your back as you plan your desert terrarium. Mentally return to the rain forest of the Washington coast which you visited last summer and think of creating one in your own home.

Bring the whole family in on the project. Plan a day when everyone searches the attic, the cellar, and the catchall closet for bottles and jars that are suitable for planting. They are just waiting there for you to give them a good scrubbing and an original arrangement of green plants. Even a six-year-old can make a terrarium and a child's enthusiasm is a delight to witness as he places his plants just where he feels they belong. I even know a burly six-foot man who has filled his bachelor apartment with terrariums he has designed and created. "In today's world of plastic credit cards and computerized programs," he told me, "people very much need to get back to the soil."

Discover for yourself how artistic you really are as you dip into your palette of fresh-smelling soils, sparkling white gravel and red-brown wood chips. Complete the picture with dabs of flower leaves and foliage color.

Start training your eye to spot the items that are available for your terrarium. Look for mosses and tiny trees in the woods, if you are fortunate enough to have them close by. Scout your neighborhood nursery and don't overlook the supermarket for healthy and inexpensive young plants.

4

Suddenly you will realize that many of those with which you are already familiar—the snake plant, the geranium, the Venus's flytrap—are adaptable to, and indeed prefer, terrarium living.

Relax and go with it. Let it be fun and a whole new vista will open for you. Don't be afraid of making a mistake, for should something go wrong it can easily be corrected. If a plant seems out of place, you can reposition it. When your vigorous dwarf palm threatens to outgrow the container, it can be trimmed back.

All kinds of experimenting are possible and then some. While there are guidelines, there are few hard and fast rules and you will find yourself innovating as you go along. If something works well for you, wonderful! If it breaks a rule, yet is successful, that's all that counts. If you learn basics, you will be able to go from there. Your terrariums will be a welcome sight to your eye and an ever-enchanting conversation piece for your home.

THE PLANTS AND I

Our walk-up apartment was well filled with plants. Mother loved them and while she did not always have the money for a new dress or a trip to the hairdresser in those post-Depression days, she did splurge on greenery. The care and attention she gave her ivies and philodendrons enabled us to enjoy them for many years.

Sunday outings were often taken by trolley car to the local botanical gardens. The warm, sweet dampness of a greenhouse can still bring back poignant memories of Mother, Dad and me, going up and down the rows of plants and flowers so beautifully arranged there for the joy of the city dweller.

At the age of ten I was allowed to do the watering of the heartier plants and the leaf shining on the sturdiest specimens. I looked on these jobs as carrying great responsibility and was proud that Mother let me do them. There were plants in each of the three rooms. On dreary winter days when the city streets were dark and deserted by 4:30 p.m., their springtime freshness added a special brightness.

I was slowly beginning to realize that a green thumb is nothing more than a desire to care for your plants, a little know-how and lots of patience and love. The plants that Mother entrusted to me were flourishing and, through the years, were putting out new pale green leaves. I was doing pretty well in this business of indoor gardening.

Then, years later, I got my first terrarium.

THAT FIRST TERRARIUM

During my novice year at teaching, a student brought me a terrarium her mother had made as a gift for me. She placed it on my desk that warm October morning. Resplendent, it was a small green world in a large glass bubble.

It was planted with ferns, mosses and a variety of woodland treats. Tiny rocks and redwood chips completed the miniature forest scene. I took it home, placed it alongside the other plants, and watered and sunned it on somewhat the same schedule as they. Within a month it was dead. I had quickly learned, if not what one *should* do, at least what one should *not* do to a terrarium. They are hearty self-contained

6

micro-worlds that survive on a lot of planned neglect and are certainly not in need of the overzealous watering I gave mine.

SOME FACTS AND FIGURES

A terrarium is a glass case with earth in it, in which plants and flowers grow. It can be of many different sizes and shapes. A common type that is easy to plant, since the top is as wide as the bottom and allows hands in, is the aquarium case. These come in a variety of sizes and can range from five gallons to twenty gallons. Two other appealing containers are the glass bubble and the brandy snifter. Their gently curving sides add beauty and line to the plants inside. Most sizes can be planted by hand; however, the smaller openings will require the use of planting tools.

The greatest challenge—and yet I think the most rewarding—is planting in a narrow-neck bottle, which can only be accomplished with special tools. Here you have to act somewhat like the scientist handling a radioactive material he can only manipulate with a pair of mechanical arms! You can see what you are doing, but you will have to think of the tools you use as extensions of your own hands, knowing they will do the job for you. Although these tools are specialized for the job, you will find you already have or can make most of the ones you will need at home.

It might seem somewhat frustrating at the beginning, and you may feel a nagging desire to reach in and set that small twig aright, or that mound of soil. Since this is not possible, you will soon learn the ways your tools can do it for you. You will find yourself placing the plant of your choice gently and yet solidly in its bed of soil. The efficient way you use the long-handled tools will have become second nature.

7

a. AQUARIUM

b. GLASS BUBBLE

c. SNIFTER

d. NARROW-NECK JAR

Figure 1. Container Silhouettes

No matter which type of glass you tackle first (and you can try all of them), the basic principles, how they work will be the same.

The purpose of any terrarium is to allow your plants and flowers to thrive in an atmosphere of controlled and constant humidity. The water needed to keep them alive and healthy and lovely to look at is provided by recycled moisture. Water vapor cools and releases its moisture when it comes in contact with the sides and top of the glass. The moisture drips down and into the soil and thus the terrarium is basically a self-watering device.

The controversy over whether to cover, not to cover, or to partially cover continues in the world of terrarium buffs. I have read of experts who say they want an airtight case. They cover their terrariums with a cork or other top and do not allow any air in. For many, this has worked well and the self-watering goes on with no problem. Others say that they want the top to be open a little to lessen the chance that mold will develop from too much moisture. There is also the alternative of covering and then opening them for some time every day or so, to allow fresh air to circulate. I have caps on all of my narrow-neck jars and they do well that way but get an occasional airing each week, or more often if the moisture is heavily beaded on the glass and the plants cannot be seen.

The owner of a local plant boutique tells me she finds a real need for covers on her glass bubbles. Ferns, so suitable in them, she says, need constant moisture and cannot be subjected to any kind of drying-out condition.

Experimenting will tell you which is the best method for you. It may be a tightly covered case or perhaps one with no cover at all, needing a more conscientious watering schedule. Usually, the narrower the neck the less need for a tight cover, as there is very little space for the moisture to escape before it "rains" back on itself in your micro-environment.

ADVANTAGES OF THE TERRARIUM

Whether you call home a cozy steam-heated city apartment or a sprawling estate in the Texas panhandle or a beach house on the Atlantic coast, a terrarium is for you. You need no longer grow plants according to the outside environment. This compact greenhouse you create will flourish anywhere. The conditions inside the jar or bottle will be just ideal and so your locale will not matter. Mosses native to South Carolina will thrive happily in a bottle garden in upper New York. Cacti from the Arizona desert can grace the living room of a family in Michigan, and the outdoors of the Vermont woods can be brought to the orange groves of Southern California.

Terrariums are excellent for apartments. They allow the high-rise dweller, who may have little time for the care and watering of his plants, to have the controlled conditions of a greenhouse under his own roof. Very inexpensively and very simply the urbanite can provide a dust-free atmosphere for his greenery. His plants will not be affected by the factory fumes drifting in the open window or the heat from the radiator that dries the air. Lack of sun is no barrier either. You will find that even in the darkest of city apartments a terrarium will grow and, given a warm glow from an overhead light, it can welcome you home at night. Nature can be captured in a glass home for any season of the year. Orchids grown in a terrarium can beautify the one-bedroom apartment.

The supplies you will need to make your terrarium are portable and easy to store. Once built, your terrarium can be moved anywhere in your house or apartment with a great deal of ease. Plants can be added at any time of the year as you will no longer be limited by the season.

Terrariums are draft free and the possibility of insect attack is limited because of the enclosure. In today's ecology-minded world, they provide one of the few rare pollution-free environments. Quick shifts in temperature will not affect the terrarium and if you turn up the heat on a snowy winter's evening your plants will not be harmed.

Your terrarium will allow you to observe the workings of nature as well as provide you with an incubator for sick plants. An aquarium planter allows for room to house these infirm ones until they are back to health. In they go, in their own pots, to recuperate in the humidity and nourishing atmosphere of the terrarium.

About the only disadvantage that I can think of is that your plants are not easily accessible to your caresses in a terrarium. If you are the type (as I am) who likes to talk sweetly to your grape ivy or gently run your fingers up and down the glossy leaves of your Schefflera, then you better leave a few plants out and in their pots for this purpose!

ABOUT THIS BOOK

Whatever your questions are about terrariums this book will answer them. You will learn of some terrarium history. All you will need in the way of tools, soil, containers, plants and flowers will be listed and explained. Ideas on how to incorporate terrariums in your own decorating scheme are given. One chapter is devoted to children, senior citizens and how terrariums can enhance their lives. Happily, you can avoid the sad fate which befell my first terrarium by reading the section on care.

You will be able to look on your very first terrarium with satisfaction and it won't be long before you will have become a master! Each new effort will be different and provide you with some fresh idea and no two will ever be exactly alike. One day you will place a strawberry begonia next to a tiny pine tree and both will take on new proportions. You could buy one, but no manner of store-bought terrarium could equal the pride you will have in caring for and enjoying something you alone have planned, prepared and planted.

CHAPTER TWO:
THE HISTORY OF
TERRARIUMS

Sir Alexander Fleming discovered penicillin by an unexpected turn of events. Charles Goodyear had no thoughts of revolutionizing America's rubber industry. Many times in the past people have attempted to invent one thing and have come upon something entirely different. What they had originally sought didn't work out but the accidental invention proved successful!

Such was the case with the first terrarium in 1829. Dr. Nathaniel Ward (Fellow of the Royal Society and Fellow of the Linnean Society) did not intend to make one, but fortunately for indoor gardeners, he did. Were Dr. Ward alive today, and able to see the far-reaching effect his happy accident has had in the world of plant growing, he would doubtlessly rejoice.

He was a lover of all the phenomena of nature surrounding his London home. Being interested in butterflies, Ward was curious to observe the emergence of the adult sphinx moth from its chrysalis. He did this by placing the clump of soil in which the chrysalis was reposing in a glass jar and covering it with a metal lid. Somewhere along the line the fate of the moth became secondary. There is disagreement among experts as to whether he ever did see it emerge and fly away as a butterfly! What began to happen to the mound of earth became more fascinating to Ward. He noticed that there were small green things growing in it. The jar had, quite by accident, become the first terrarium.

These green growths excited Ward, for many times before he had tried and failed to grow plants on an old wall outside of his home. The impure air of London, with its smoke and dirt, prevented him from doing this. Now, here were ferns and grasses thriving in this enclosed case. They stayed alive and healthy in this jar for almost four years until rain seeped in and waterlogged the soil while Ward was away from home. This was unfortunate, as it would have proved interesting to see how much longer they might have lasted without care, water or attention.

Ward became intrigued with this method of keeping plants. He grew ferns in wide-mouth jars and covered some with bell jars. One of his experiments, the growing of an extremely tricky fern, the filmy fern, was so successful that it grew fronds fifteen inches long, longer than those it put out in its native habitat. Eventually it outgrew the container and had to be taken to a fern house.

Ward continued to grow things under glass and covered with glass. Much of his experimenting was done with ferns which need the constant humidity a terrarium provides. He planted palms, ferns, mosses, aloes and cacti in glass enclosures. Montague Free in his book, *All About House Plants,* quotes Ward: "The palms have now been enclosed for fifteen years. . . they will continue for many years without outgrowing their natural bounds."

In an 8' x 8' case he constructed for the north side of his house, Ward was even able to grow ferns and cacti together by having the cacti suspended from a bar on the top. Thus, they got a minimum of water. The ferns were put on the bottom where more moisture was available to them.

In 1842, Ward wrote a book called *On The Growth of Plants in Closely Glazed Cases.* This was probably the first book ever written on the subject of terrariums. It is noted that Ward was able to maintain a bottle of ferns and mosses in perfect shape without watering for eighteen years.

Subsequent use was being made of glass containers for house plants. They were utilized to transplant tropical plants on long sea voyages and were crudely constructed glass boxes which carried exotic plants. When Ward began to publicize the use of glass enclosures for plant growing, his Wardian case could be seen gracing Victorian homes. Indeed, some English historians have said that these glass cases were a craze. Today we are experiencing a renewed interest in them. In the late 1800s all manner of ornate glass was used to display plants. Ferns under glass were very popular and many of the bell jars we now see in antique shops housing stuffed birds were originally used for plants and terrariums.

Dr. Nathaniel Ward stumbled upon and perfected a way of growing plants under glass. (Many reference books still allude to glass gardens as Wardian Cases.) You can take advantage of the knowledge gleaned from his chance discovery to make and enjoy your own terrariums.

CHAPTER THREE: SUPPLIES AND TOOLS FOR MAKING TERRARIUMS

Sometimes starting a new hobby or expanding an already established one necessitates buying varied and expensive tools and supplies. More often than we would like, many of them will not be used and our money was spent unnecessarily. This is not the case with terrarium making. All of your supplies and tools will be relatively inexpensive and will pay for themselves in the hours of use and enjoyment you will get from the finished product. Too, they are portable and do not require an inordinate amount of storage space. A closet or shelf can house them all.

One of the most useful tools for bottle garden planting, the wire hanger, is found in goodly supply in your closet. I have recently spoken to a young terrarium merchant who bought his tools at first but eventually he constructed his own. He claims he feels much more comfortable about using these than the store-bought ones! Basically, his tools are made from hangers and bits and pieces of rubber and sponge.

Some of the other items you will need—charcoal, potting soil, gravel—may also be close at hand. Your most versatile tools for planting the wider-mouth jars and cases are your own two hands. However, in the case of the narrow-neck wine jug or water bottle, your imagination can help you fashion a tool which will work just perfectly. Trial, and perhaps error, will show you the ones that are best for you. The tools and supplies mentioned in this chapter are suggestions and have been found to work well. You may find something entirely different that will meet your exact needs. In terrarium-making as in many other areas, necessity will become the mother of invention.

TOOLS

The right tool to do the right job is most important in any task. For making a terrarium there are many right tools. Some are especially for use in the narrow-neck bottles. These will be listed and explained. Some are for both the narrow neck and the hands-in top and these will be discussed. The function of a tool will be listed—the job it is to do—and suggestions made as to which tool could be used to do each job.

Your first concern will be the preparation of the soil bed on the bottom of the container. Placement of soil in large-mouth jars can be done by hand. In the narrow-neck bottle you will need a *funnel* of some sort.

Funnel

This can be anything that is narrow enough to get into the neck of the bottle and yet wide enough to allow pouring of gravel and soil through it. The funnel should carry material almost to the bottom of the bottle or jar. If it doesn't, there is a chance the dirt will get on the sides of the glass and it is difficult to clean off. It is best to avoid letting dirt adhere to the sides of the bottle.

Funnels can be:

1. A cardboard roller such as those from inside a roll of paper towels or gift wrapping.

2. A piece of heavy paper or bendable cardboard, rolled and fastened with staples or tape.

3. A small plastic or metal funnel that can be placed at the top of the cardboard roller to make a wider top and avoid spillage.

Your next concern will be to dig the holes in which the plants will be placed. Here again, if your hand fits in, you can do it with your fingers or a spoon. If not, some kind of *shovel* device is needed.

Shovel

Suggested shovels are:

1. A long-handled iced tea or demitasse spoon if the container opening will accommodate it.

2. A piece of round curtain rod about 1/2" in diameter.

3. A pencil or wooden dowel long enough to get to the soil and poke a hole in it. (The other end of the dowel can be used as a tamping tool.)

4. A garden stake, such as those used for tomato plants.

5. A chopstick.

Placer

Next you will need a *placer*. (These are needed only for the narrower-necked containers.) Their function is to hold the plant while you lower it into the container and place it in the hole you have prepared for it in the soil bed. There are many which work well and you will find the best for you in a short time.

1. The least expensive and probably the easiest to make is the coat-hanger placer. The hanger is straightened out and then a loop is made on the bottom to hold the plant. The roots go through the loop and the top of the plant sits on the top of the loop. Or a length of copper wiring may be looped the same way.

2. A pickup tool can be bought at a hardware store. These are really wire pullers and have retractable prongs on one end of a long stick. When these are open you can place the plant in them and then close them around the plant and lower it to the bottom of the bottle.

Once the roots are put in the hole and secured, you can release these prongs by operating the upper end of the tool and let the plant stay where it is. (These work like a clam on a steam shovel.)

The placer is an essential tool because it has to get the plants to the bottom. Should it fail to work well—if the plant drops out of it—it is hard to right it again. The placer must hold the plant firmly yet allow for easy releasing once the

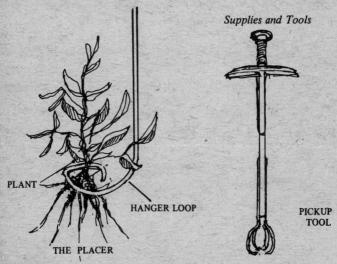

PLANT

HANGER LOOP

PICKUP
TOOL

THE PLACER

Figure 2. *Planting Tools*

plant has been tamped in place. For the wider-top containers, a pair of kitchen tongs can work as a placer.

Tamper

Once the hole is dug and the plant placed, you will need a *tamper* to secure it in the soil. In large-top containers you can do this with your fingers; in the narrow-neck ones, a tool is used. In tamping, take care that the soil is placed gently around the roots but that they are well-covered and solidly in.

Suggested tampers are:

1. A wooden dowel with a cork attached to one end. (Use the other end of your dowel shovel for this.) Cut a small hole with a pocket knife in the wider end of the cork and glue it to the end of the dowel. The soft cork will not damage the roots as you tamp them down.

2. Attach a small piece of rubber or sponge to a straightened hanger.

3. Insert a small piece of rubber into one end of a glass straw or pipette.

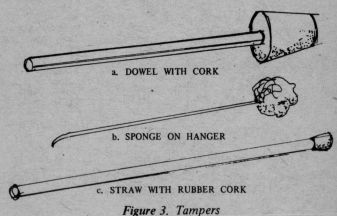

a. DOWEL WITH CORK

b. SPONGE ON HANGER

c. STRAW WITH RUBBER CORK

Figure 3. Tampers

Tweezer

After your plants are placed and secured, clean up any debris at the bottom of the container. You can do this with a *tweezer* that can be used in all kinds of containers. Tweezers are also used for placing any finishing touches—redwood chips, rocks, moss—you may wish to add.

Examples of tweezers are:

1. A bamboo stake slit about halfway up. Wedge a piece of wood in the angle and tie with string or a rubber band.

2. A long-handled tweezer such as the type bought in a secondhand medical supply store or long-handled aquarium tweezers.

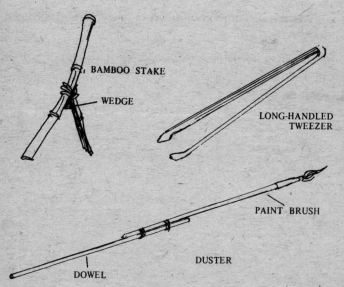

BAMBOO STAKE

WEDGE

LONG-HANDLED TWEEZER

PAINT BRUSH

DUSTER

DOWEL

Figure 4. Cleaning Tools

Cleaner and Duster

Your terrarium is almost complete. You will need a *cleaner* for any dirt that may have gotten on the glass as you were working. Wipe the outside clean with a soft damp cloth and then dry. You can use this method for the inside of the larger openings. However, in the narrow-neck containers you will need a bottle brush, which can be curved to fit the sides of the jar.

You will need some sort of *duster* to clean the leaves, which may have become dirty while planting.

1. This is done with a small soft-bristled paint brush. If it is

not long enough to reach to the bottom of the container, you can tie it to a dowel end.

2. A cotton-tipped swab will work in the larger-mouthed containers to swab the leaves.

Watering Devices

The initial amount of *watering* of the terrarium is essential. You will not want it too wet. Yet there has to be a fair amount of soil water to start with.

Watering devices are:

1. A bulb sprayer.

2. A kitchen baster.

3. A laundry sprayer or plant spray bottle.

4. A long-necked funnel that will reach down the sides and to the soil of a narrow-neck container.

Pruner

Although it is wise to prune yellow or dying leaves before planting, you may find that some will yellow after they are planted. To *prune* plants once they are in the terrarium use a device that will enable you to take off the leaves you do not want cleanly and efficiently. Your pruner will also be helpful for thinning plants that looked small a few months ago but now threaten to take over the entire container.

For pruning use:

1. Small manicure scissors in wide-top container.

2. Long, thin scissors for narrow-neck bottles.

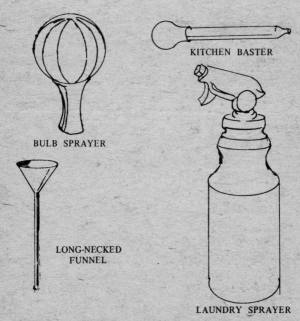

Figure 5. *Watering Devices*

3. Single-edge razor blade taped to a dowel.

4. A paper clip curved on the end of a bamboo stake—to remove debris.

Pruning can also be done by removing the entire plant, pruning it and then replanting it. This is easiest if you can get your hands in the container. Otherwise you may run into difficulty trying to extricate one plant without disturbing the others. But do try it. You may be more successful at it than I!

Soil Tester

A device to *test* the soil for moisture at the bottom of the container may be used. This can be the other end of your glass pipette or straw tamp. Push it into the soil, pull some up, and inspect the clod for dampness.

WHERE TO OBTAIN THE TOOLS

Tools you have at home or can make:

1. Wire hanger placer
2. Cardboard or heavy paper funnel
3. Iced tea or demitasse spoons
4. Curtain rod—about 12" piece 1/2" in diameter
5. Pencil
6. Chopstick
7. Cloth pieces
8. Manicure scissors
9. Long thin scissors
10. Paper clip
11. Single-edge razor blade
12. Soft-bristle paint brush
13. Cotton-tipped swab
14. Bulb syringe
15. Baster
16. Laundry or plant spray bottle
17. Kitchen tongs
18. Small pieces of rubber and sponge

TOOLS TO BUY AND APPROXIMATE PRICES

Tool	Price	Where to Buy
1. Small funnel	29¢	Hardware store
2. Dowel	15¢	Hardware store, lumber yard
3. Cork	3¢ – 6¢	Hardware store
4. Garden Stake	79¢ pack.	Nursery
5. Pickup tools	99¢	Hardware store
6. Long-handled tweezer	Varied	Medical supply store
7. Copper wire	By length	Hardware store
8. Glass straw or pipette	$1.00	Hardware store
9. Aquarium tweezers	$1.98	Aquarium store
10. Bottle brush under	$1.00	Art supply store or Hobby shop

PLANTING MATERIALS

Most terrariums require the same general planting bed. In the desert terrarium, however, you will add more sand. You will need:

Soil: Any good sterilized package mix will do for the soil. There are many excellent ones on the market today, and they come in a variety of sizes and prices. I use the 2-1/2 pound size, as it is manageable to carry and yet there is enough soil in it for at least 1/2 dozen large size terrariums. If the planting mix is too rich it will make your plants grow leggy and thus defeat the purpose of a terrarium—to allow for slow, even growth. The ingredients in the package mix I use are:

27

Redwood leaf mold
Forest humus
Aqua-sorb
Peat moss
Oak leaf mold
Peat humus
Humusite
Charcoal
Perlite

and it is blended with "sponge-rok."

You will notice that the soil contains an airing material—perlite—and some charcoal for sweetening. Black Magic and Supersoil are both excellent house plant mixtures. This soil feels light and airy to the touch and yet it is able to retain its body. The airiness allows the roots of your terrarium plants to breathe.

Two recipes for making your own soil are:

I
One part sand
One part topsoil
One part leaf mold or peat moss

II
Two parts fresh topsoil
One part sand
One part leafmold, compost or well-rotted cow manure
Some charcoal

Mix either of these recipes and put through a sieve to get the texture of the soil needed for your terrarium. Add more sand for the desertarium and more loam for planting ferns and mosses.

If there are no drainage holes at the bottom of your container you will need crushed rock or gravel. Use well-washed aquarium gravel or buy packaged white or colored decorator rock. A 2-1/2 pound package at 39¢ can be used for six terrariums.

This drainage material is very important. Without it the soil in your terrarium would become water-logged and the plants would die from lack of root air. You may wish to add a few small pieces of charcoal for sweetening. A briquette from your barbecue will work well if it is broken up into bite-sized pieces. To line the container, buy sheet or sphagnum moss at a nursery.

MATERIALS NEEDED FOR FINISHING TOUCHES

Depending on your personal preference, you may or may not choose to add some small ceramic figures to the terrarium. In most of the store-bought ones you will notice a small brown snail reposing on a bed of moss or an impish green elf peeking around a miniature pine tree. These are commercial touches and help to sell terrariums. Indeed, I was told by a nursery worker that people often actually choose a terrarium for the animal in it and pay no attention to the appearance or health of the plants! Whether you are a purist or add a chipmunk or squirrel is entirely up to you. Other more natural touches are redwood chips, small rocks and shiny stones.

Ceramic figurines cost under $1.00 at most stationery stores. Tiny gates and bridges are also available, and these can be used in woodland scenes, should you feel the desire for them.

CHAPTER FOUR: ALL ABOUT CONTAINERS

Four: All About Containers

A strange thing will begin to happen once you become interested in terrarium making...you will find yourself buying liquids to get the containers in which they come! There is a particular juice on the market which does not please my family's taste, but it does come in an interesting bottle. So we endure drinking it to get those bottles! Other desirable terrarium planters are wine jugs. Choose those made of clear glass with narrow necks. If you do not partake of the juice of the grape, find a friend or neighbor who does and ask him to save the bottles for you.

That fish bowl the children no longer use will be adaptable for your new hobby. Even peanut butter jars with wide tops can hold a small fern or two. And the cookie jar, which has long since been relegated to the back of the closet, makes a fine glass house.

Your eye will quickly become trained and wherever you look you will see glass containers suitable for planting. Once you are in the market for them, you will notice jars and bottles almost everywhere.

GLASS OR PLASTIC

Originally, terrariums were made only of glass. Today it is possible to buy one made of plastic. Department stores advertise large plastic bubbles with dome tops in a do-it-yourself terrarium kit, complete with directions for planting. The more pleasing ones to me, however, are those made from glass. Plastic has an artificial look, which detracts from the desired "natural" effect of the scene. If you do not feel this way, try the plastic cake dome or a large clear plastic salad bowl. Search and experiment to learn what pleases your eye.

Whatever you choose to plant in, there are several facts to consider. It is best to find a clear glass container that will allow for maximum viewing pleasure. Sometimes there is writing on a jar or bottle. If it is not too prominent it will not obscure the plants. You may also find bottles with a design or picture etched in them. These bottles may distort what is inside. If possible collect containers with nothing imprinted on them. Inspect for holes and cracks that could cause leakage and damage to table tops.

You should consider what you will be planting in any particular container when choosing it. Plants that like lots of humidity will be happiest in covered containers or narrow-neck bottles. Desert plants, which like dry conditions, will do well in open tops. If you wish to use a glass bubble without a top, choose plants that do not require a constant high humidity. The more open the top, the less humidity; so plant accordingly.

WIDE-TOP CONTAINERS

Any container with at least a 4" mouth may be planted by hand. These include aquarium cases, snifters and bubbles. Start with one of these if you've never tried your hand at a terrarium before. They can be done quickly and simply and with stunning results.

AQUARIUM-TYPE PLANTERS

The largest top openings are those on aquariums. These are excellent for terrariums and easy to plant as there is ample room for you to get both hands in and work with your plants. Aquarium cases range in size from the two gallon to the twenty-nine gallon size. Approximate retail prices for an empty aquarium container are:

2 gallon — $4.99
5 gallon — $6.50
10 gallon — $10.50
20 gallon — $20.99
29 gallon — $33.99

An aquarium case can be constructed at home. Use a

wooden box of 4 or 5 inches high as a base. Make the side supports of wood or aluminum. The dimensions can vary although a good size is 14" x 10" x 8". Have a glazier cut the sides for you and seal them to the wood or aluminum. A cover that is a little larger than the top will be adequate. If the bottom of the box is slatted, this will allow for drainage. If it is not, you may want to have 1/4" holes bored in it.

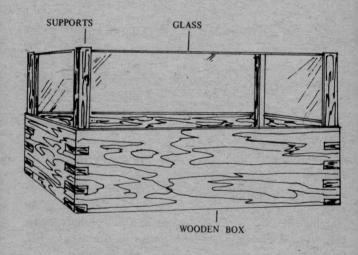

SUPPORTS   GLASS

WOODEN BOX

Figure 6. Aquarium to Construct

BRANDY SNIFTERS

Brandy snifters remind me of romantic old movies with the hero leaning on the mantle gently twirling an after-dinner drink in this oversized glass! These ovate vessels are excellent for terrariums and are sold in many liquor stores. Their tops are large and most sizes will allow for hands-in planting.

Snifters are sold by their capacity in ounces. The smaller one hundred-ounce size can accommodate five plants without crowding and the large 820-ounce size holds twelve plants comfortably. Prices for empty snifters vary. I have seen some for as low as $1.99 for one hundred-ounce size and as high as $19.98 for the large size. Thickness and quality of the glass will determine the price. Hunt for secondhand ones at salvage stores and garage sales. A good scrubbing may be all they will need to make them sparkle. Most do not have covers, but it is possible for you to have one cut at a glazier or you can stretch a piece of plastic wrap over the opening.

GLASS BUBBLES

Glass bubbles are very pleasing to the eye when used as terrariums. Their rounded sides allow for unimpeded viewing of plants and flowers. They bulge out gently through the middle and provide growing room for young plants. Bubbles are measured across the fattest part of their middle. Those that measure eight inches across the middle are fine for planting five small plants and larger sixteen-inch bubbles are able to hold twelve plants. Other sizes measure ten inches, twelve inches and fourteen inches across the middle.

A bubble may be covered or uncovered. If you are using plants that enjoy high humidity, it is wise to have a cover made. Some bubbles can be bought with a peaked top cover, which keeps the moisture content high.

DOME COVERINGS

An extremely attractive and easy way to make a terrarium is to place a glass or plastic dome over a planted dish or bowl. What is important here is that the dome must fit exactly over the sides of the dish so that a tight seal is achieved. You may have seen domes covering waxed fruit or other keepsakes. (When I was a child my grandmother had such a glass dome which she used to cover the iced decoration of her twenty-fifth wedding anniversary cake.) Interestingly, these domes were probably used in Victorian days to cover plants and ferns, then later for mementos, and now they are back again and being used for their original purpose.

A dome is a delightful way to display plants. The arched top allows for a tall, striking plant to be the focal point. Even one regal palm will look lovely under a dome. There need be little else with it—perhaps only some moss or a small rock at the base.

Domes are easy to plant. You can make your whole arrangement in the dish or bowl and then place the dome over it. Plantings under domes are easily accessible to rearrangement and trimming.

OTHER WIDE TOPS

Also suitable for terrariums are:

Large restaurant-size mayonnaise jars (2 gallon capacity)

Five-gallon wide-mouth jars
Glass pantry or cookie jars
Apothecary jars
Candy jars with wide tops

Recently I saw some terrariums in hollow glass bricks used as supports for wooden shelves. The "waviness" of the glass did somewhat distort the plants inside and I wondered about the stability of the entire structure. Perhaps planted glass bricks would better be left on a table top.

The possibilities are endless. Jean Hersey in her book, *Garden in Your Window,* describes how she removed the insides from a 150-watt light bulb after its end had been broken off. It adequately housed ferns and other tiny green things on her desk!

MORE CHALLENGING CONTAINERS

When choosing a narrow-neck container for planting, find one with a neck at least wide enough to ease a plant through. The large-size wine jugs are fine for your bottle planting. Also try juice or vinegar jars. A quart-size salad oil bottle is another inexpensive possibility. Acid carboys are excellent. Even cider jugs, pickle jars and kerosene bottles look handsome when planted. A very popular container today is the distilled water jug. Most have a five-gallon capacity and can be planted and set on the floor or a table, either upright or on their sides. Unfortunately some are imprinted with the distributor's name and others are too darkly tinted, but many are useable. If you can find a distributor who will get a clear, unetched one for you, it will probably cost about $2.00.

I have seen a number of large glass pumpkins made into terrariums, and small test tubes holding five-leafed ferns. All manner of narrow-neck containers are a worthwhile challenge in terrarium making.

The enclosure in which you place your plants and flowers is important to your whole design plan. Whether you choose a wide top or a narrow-neck water jug will depend on many things. The size and shape of the container will have a bearing on the type and number of plants that will go into it. Let the glass house enhance its occupants. What may look wonderful under a dome would not be right in a wine jug. Experiment with placement before you actually plant in any container. It is easier to move a potted plant than one already embedded at the bottom of a bottle.

If you like the line and feel of a particular jar unplanted, chances are you will enjoy it planted. If not, look for something more pleasing to you. Do not spend time and energy planting a container that does not suit your fancy to begin with!

WHERE TO FIND THE CONTAINERS

Terrarium-makers never know when they are going to come upon a suitable jar for planting. The other day I was in a neighbor's backyard and saw a fantastic large-mouth jar hanging from a hook in an unused stable! It is perfectly suited for a floor terrarium. Scout the local junkyards and antique stores for secondhand decanters and bottles. Remember, for your terrarium they can have a small imperfection; so you may be able to pick them up quite inexpensively.

Chemical supply houses are sources for used acid carboys. (*Carboy* is an ancient term for a glass container that was placed in a basket for transporting chemicals on ships.) Today wood is put around the carboy, and when the crate becomes broken from use the bottle is sold as is. They come in sizes from five gallons to thirteen gallons and cost $2.00 each.

Visits to flea markets, secondhand shops and garage sales will uncover a wealth of inexpensive bottles suitable for planting. Liquor stores and markets, backyards and basements—all are places to unearth miniature greenhouses. Stores are featuring terrarium planters "scientifically designed for indoor atmosphere to insure healthy growth of plants." All manner of jars, jugs, bottles, dishes and domes are at your fingertips. What houses your *vin rose* today can be your terrarium tomorrow and where your pickles once reposed will be planted your pilea!

CHAPTER FIVE:
GREEN PLANTS
FOR THE TERRARIUM

Choosing plants for your terrarium will prove a delightful and challenging job. Will they be small with dark green leaves or will the lacy look of a fern catch your fancy? Mix and match when you pick your plants, but just be sure that they need similar growing conditions.

It is wise to consider the temperature and moisture requirements of the plants that will share the same terrarium. An Old Man cactus will not do as well with as much moisture as your prayer plant; so put them in separate containers. Wet and dry plants do best if they are not together in the same bottle garden. Know which plants need a closed container with high humidity, which a partially open one, and which an uncovered one. (There are also some plants that will grow almost anywhere!) Although plants that require very humid conditions are terrarium favorites, do not exclude others that want less wetness. They can go into an open-top terrarium for more air and less moisture.

Decide where the completed terrarium will be placed. If it is to be in a sunny location, try succulents. If it will grace your bathroom counter and receive coolness and shade, then use mosses and ferns. These, incidentally, are well suited to a terrarium lifestyle since they were around millions of years ago when much of our world was still a swamp with a moist, humid atmosphere. Group those plants that want coolness together away from those that thrive in a warmer environment.

No matter if you are buying the plantings or gathering them in the woods, decide on plants you like. Select ones you were afraid to try before because they were difficult to tend. Terrariums turn everyone's thumbs green!

SIZE, COLOR AND TEXTURE

I have found that the size of a plant can be rather deceptive. What looks small enough to be contained in that narrow-neck bottle can actually be too large for it once it is inside! I have bought plants I loved, only to get them home and find they are already too bountiful for my wine jug. It is a good idea to take your container along when buying plants and place it next to them for sizing. Sometimes you may have to prune before planting and sometimes you may have to search for a larger jar. The size of the case should be a factor in choosing your plants. Since everything grows well and quickly in a terrarium, make sure you are not planting a green thing that will engulf all the other green things in its path before too long. If you adore that palm plant, inquire first if it will need more growing room than the decanter you have chosen for it. When it's fully grown will it outgrow its house entirely?

For the more vertical plants such as crotons, umbrella plants and asparagus ferns you will need a taller container. Take into consideration, too, the growth habits of the plant. Will it spread out and fill the sides of the bowl in a pleasing display? Or a tangled mass?

Medium height plants include Chinese evergreen, fittonias, pileas, and small-leafed ivies.

Examples of smaller plants are: ferns in the Pteris family, grape ivy and boxwood shoots.

Since plants grow superfast in the terrarium atmosphere, it is best to stay with small pot sizes. Young plants in 2-1/2" pots (at 49¢ each) are the most sensible. If you have an extremely large bowl, 3" pots may be used with discretion. Don't crowd your plants. Allow them breathing and growing room. You want your terrarium to look well planned, not like an overgrown area of the jungle. One fern alone will be more effective than many, all pushing and poking their way through the top of the bottle.

Green plants come in a variety of shades. Leaves and foliage colors range from the palest, softest greens to the deepest near-black tones. Place the brightest and sharpest leaves next to those whose colors are more subdued for a striking effect. Certain leaves are smooth, others have ridges and markings. Contrast a glossy silk-like leaf with a furry or variegated one.

PLANT SOURCES

No longer is a buyer restricted to a florist's shop or nursery for green plants. "Pockets of Greenery" are seen in markets, gift shops, and department stores. Plant boutiques offer a mind-boggling array of foliage, including young potted plants, perfect specimens for the terrarium. Stroll through one of these places and see what is available to you. Talk to others and learn what has worked well for them. Take advantage of the knowledgeable storekeepers who can assist you in the selection and care of your plants. Boutique owners consider each plant their child, and do not turn any over to you without specific instructions on care and feeding!

Should you live near the woods or a meadow where you are allowed to pick and gather, do so. Be absolutely certain that it is legal to uproot the moss, fern or the small twig of ivy. If so, you have a perfect source for plants you can take home and put in your terrarium. Naturally, not all plants are available in all regions of the country. Today, however, due to improved transportation, you will be able to get many by mail order that may not be native to your locale. In the controlled environment of a terrarium, they will flourish.

If you have a favorite potted plant at home, it is often possible to snip off a piece, root it in water and then plant it in the terrarium. Even patches of grass from your lawn can reflect beauty under glass. The important factors—the humidity, the temperature, and the light the plants need—should be your guidelines in choosing which ones will go in the same terrarium. Experimentation will guide you more and more as you go along. Discover what does well for you. There is a wealth of greenery—woodland plants, tropicals, cacti and succulents and even carniverous ones—all awaiting you.

WOODLAND PLANTS

Taking a walk in the woods can be a fascinating botanical experience! Mosses, ferns, Selaginellas and country lichens—all there to capture your eye. Any of these will thrive in the moist atmosphere of a terrarium. If you are allowed to do so, take home plants from the woods, the forest or the park. Bring along a trowel or small shovel and dig the specimen you desire, leaving a large clump of soil around the roots. Sprinkle plants to keep them moist and take them home in a plastic bag. (Last summer on a walk through the Hoh Rain Forest in Washington, I saw myriads of mosses and ferns. However, in these national parks the rule is to take only photographs, so I simply looked with longing!)

Even if you live in a large city, train your eye to find mosses growing near the exposed roots of trees. Excavation sites can also prove to be fruitful digging grounds.

Woodland plants require a rich soil and no direct sunlight. They will do best in a cool room or sun porch. If you have walked through a rain forest and seen the mosses and ferns in their natural surroundings you will notice that they are usually in filtered sunlight or shade. These temperate-zone plants like coolness. Mosses do not bloom but will carpet your terrarium in green. Lichens, found only in the country, make charming additions to the terrarium. Green-grey fairy cups and red-tipped lichens grow near cut and rotting trees. If you can gather some for your terrarium, they will be a very special part of the woodland scene.

FERNS

Ferns, many so fragile and dainty that they are almost impossible to keep alive at home, are practically fool-proof in the terrarium. The constant mist gives these woodland plants an atmosphere close to the one they grow in naturally. One even hears the term "terrarium fern" applied to a small filmy fern.

You may order ferns from suppliers or gather your own. A good way to take them home from the woods is in a small waxed milk container. Run a knife under the roots of the fern as close to the rock as possible and then put this blanket into the container. It is important that you keep the soil wet and give it a good soaking before planting in the terrarium. Select small varieties of ferns for your terrarium. Some of them can grow as tall as fifty feet and would hardly be suitable for your apothecary jar! Ferns need light, perfect drainage, high humidity, and a rich acidy soil. Those you can choose for your woodland terrarium are:

Maidenhair ferns — These are excellent terrarium plants. The Southern Maidenhair grows in abundance on coquina rocks in Florida in constant moisture. Maidenhair ferns are almost never successful unless grown in the terrarium for they must constantly have moisture-laden air.

Rock fern — This fern is found mostly on boulders and ledges.

Rattlesnake fern — A fern with criss-crossed white veins on its leaves that will add interest to the terrarium. These do well in a moderate amount of moisture.

Ebony spleenwort — These ferns like shade and not too acidy soil. Fine for covered terrariums, their feathery fronds are lovely under glass and easy to grow.

Oak fern — This fern does well in the dampness of a terrarium.

Bird's Nest fern — When the leaves first appear, in the heart of the plant, they are oval and resemble bird eggs in a nest. They uncurl to become bright green and leathery in appearance.

Holly fern — The holly fern will do well in less humidity and more heat than other ferns. Its foliage resembles that of Christmas holly. It can grow quite large; so choose a container of ample size.

Victorian fern — This fern, with silver-striped foliage, will stay small and adds a light, wispy feel to the terrarium.

Button fern — Round leaves and dark stems make this fern highly decorative.

Other ferns suited for the terrarium are: the hedge fern, the ribbon fern, and the walking fern.

SELAGINELLAS

These are a higher form of plant life than the fern, and are sometimes considered in the tropical family, although some will thrive in cooler conditions than tropical plants. They are similar to mosses in that their creeping, low species make excellent ground covers for the terrarium. You may sometimes see these called moss ferns and, like the ferns, they like moisture.

MOSSES

Mosses are available in many different varieties. They do well in the terrarium as any dryness makes them lifeless. Club mosses are primitive plants that will remain low throughout life and are well suited for glass enclosures. Mosses grow on rocks and stone as well as on earth and trees. Brown sphagnum moss from Louisiana is fine for lining your terrarium and giving it a decorative touch. Excellent as ground cover, mosses come in a variety of hair lengths and frond patterns. Some are smooth, others rough. And color varies. Look for mosses in the woods. Many are there for the taking. Helxine soleiroli (or baby's tears) makes a fine ground cover and stays low. Its twiggy branches will spread out on the bottom of the terrarium with a moss-like appearance.

TREES IN THE TERRARIUM

Tiny trees will not only look charming in the natural world of the terrarium but will stay small for a surprisingly long time. Dwarf evergreen, small pine and sprouting acorns gathered in the fall can be put into a terrarium to enjoy for the winter season. Miniature varieties of cypress, spruce, hemlock, yew and fir are other possibilities. One well-placed tree under a glass dome can be a complete woodland scene. Seedlings of hemlock and spruce have lovely feathery foliage.

TROPICAL PLANTS

Their very name implies that these plants want a warmer atmosphere than those of the woodland variety. They require heat and moisture and will do well in the terrarium under somewhat different conditions than the woodland species.

The African violet is especially suited to the terrarium. Try different varieties of these in miniature and regular size. You will discover that under glass they are easy to care for and succeed in this greenhouse-like atmosphere.

Pileas and peperomias

Particularly adaptable for terrarium growing are plants in the *Pilea* and peperomia families. They remain low and their colored and carved leaves provide interest.

Pilea involucrata — The deeply quilted leaves of this plant are green on top and red underneath. Miniature flowers grow which seem to be resting on the leaves. Care should be taken that it is kept small.

Pilea cadierei minima — This plant is also known as the aluminum plant because of shiny leaf markings.

Pilea depressa — Has round fleshy leaves and remains low.

Peperomia sandersi — Often referred to as the watermelon plant, this peperomia has silver bands that radiate from the center of each leaf.

Peperomia obtusifolia minima — The variegated leaves on this plant add interest to the terrarium arrangement.

Peperomia caperata — With deeply furrowed leaves this plant is also called the emerald ripple.

Other tropicals

Other tropical plants to consider for the terrarium are:

The Prayer Plant — Since this plant does well in the humidity of the bathroom, it is especially adaptable to a terrarium. It likes warmth but never strong sun and is so named because the leaves move up at dusk as if in prayer. The maranta family, of which this plant is a member, all need humid conditions.

The Nerve Plant — This plant, with its oval leaves veined in white, does well in the moistness of the terrarium. It belongs to the fittonias, and they enjoy humid conditions. The nerve plant will grow low and will trail.

Begonia — There are many varieties of these. The smaller-leafed ones do best in the terrarium.

Philodendron — Select the smaller varieties of these hardy tropical vines for under-glass planting.

Dracaena sanderiana — This plant has slim graceful leaves striped with white. I warn you, however, it may outgrow its confines sooner than you would desire. It can be cut back at the base and will grow another stem.

Dwarf palm — Most palms will grow quite large, but the dwarf variety can be contained under glass.

CACTUS AND OTHER SUCCULENTS

These easy-to-obtain and easy-to-grow plants are for the more open top terrarium or desertarium. Since they do not need constant moisture—many want very little at all—they may be left open to the air and sun. Cacti, almost exclusively American, and succulents, native to Africa, require the same dry environment and both have facilities for storing water. The cacti retain it in their thick stems while the succulents' fleshy leaves hold it. Squeeze the leaf of a succulent and you can readily see the water.

Cacti offer many varieties from which to choose. Their growth indoors can be limited and care is minimal. Some will need occasional watering with room-temperature water. Few cacti have any leaves because they would cause too much water evaporation. After a resting period in a cool place in winter, cacti can be set out in a south window in direct sunlight for the summer months. Together in a glass bowl, cacti and succulents present an unusual contrast of texture and color.

Examples of cacti for a desertarium are:

Old man cactus — This variety got its name because of long waving hair which comes from the top of its thick stem.

Bishop's cap — Shaped like a five-ribbed bishop's cap this cactus puts out a yellow flower on its top.

Other cacti small enough for the terrarium are: bunny ear, tiger jaw and sand dollar.

Examples of succulents for the desertarium are: jade plant, kalanchoe, aloe, seedling gasteria, the Sedum (live-forever) and the miracle leaf or air plant.

For your desertarium take care to choose the smaller species of cacti and succulents. Use a sandy soil and keep it dry in winter and moist in summer.

SURPRISE PLANTINGS

When you plant a seed or a clump of moss it will sprout into plants unknown! The grab-bag terrarium you bring home from the outdoors is full of surprises. Plants already established are less fun than watching an acorn in a bottle show the beginnings of a forest oak. Many seeds will also do well in your terrarium. A pinch of grass seed will shortly become a little tuft of lawn. Drop an orange seed in the earth and observe its small shiny leaves begin to push up. Cultivate herbs in a glass jar—thyme for use in poultry stuffing, sweet basil for eggs, parsley for garnishing. Be sure to weed out the weakest growths.

GROUND COVERS

After you have planted, fill in open spaces to give a feeling of unity to the entire picture. Ground covers that stay low and are suggested as fillers include:

Baby's tears
Crinkle-leaf peperomia
Selaginellas
Moss—Living sheet moss, sphagnum moss from marshes
    or dried decorators moss
Wandering Jew
Strawberry begonia

PART II
MAKING
THE
TERRARIUM

CHAPTER SIX:
COLOR COMES
TO THE TERRARIUM

However lovely the ivy grows or the palm flourishes, there will be a time when you will want color in your terrarium. Color gives new life to otherwise quiet spots in the house and can put one in a bright mood no matter how dark the day. Flowering plants are only one of the many ways in which color can be introduced into your terrarium. There are plants whose leaves have individual color variation—reds, pinks, and soft browns. Colorful trailers and creepers are plentiful and grow low to fit the confines of a glass container. Buds can be forced to blossom under glass long before their outdoor blooming season is upon you. Budded twigs add color, as will lily of the valley "pips" when grown in a glass decanter. If you have a fluorescent growing light it is even possible to make flowers blossom forth in a closet or the darkest corner of a bedroom. Tiny trees tinged with silver, red and blue-green also provide color accents for the terrarium.

PLANTS WHOSE FLOWERS PROVIDE COLOR

African violets — These lush velvety tropical house plants are an all-time favorite. They are ideal for humid terrariums and put out flowers from the purest white to the deepest reds and purples. Use a commercial African violet soil mix for planting and, with just one crown in a glass bubble, a scene of serene beauty can be achieved. They like light, but only filtered sunlight. Remove cover for some time each day for air circulation.

Miniature roses — Roses are a universally enjoyed flower. Well-tended blooming rose gardens are always a joy to see. (I know of a rather ordinary house that has a breathtaking rose garden in the front yard, and that has always been its emotional selling point.) If you haven't room for an outdoor garden during the winter season, there are miniatures you can grow under glass. The Rosa Rouletti was the first of these delightful small roses to be discovered. A Swiss, Dr. Roulet, first discovered them growing in cottage windows in the village of Mauborget, Switzerland. Reports indicated that they had been growing there for centuries as a house plant. The fairy or pygmy rose (*Rosa Chinensis Minima*), the red imp and the yellow miniature are some you can grow indoors. Roses, in or out of doors, like sun. Under glass, they need moisture and a daily airing.

Miniature geraniums — Perfect for growing under glass, these small flowering delights need an airing each day and a moist soil. Plant in equal parts of sand and garden soil. Tiny enough to grow even under a water glass, the pigmy geranium has red flowers and the pixie geraniums are salmon-pink. They will need some sun to bloom and show their range of colors from white to deep red.

Begonias — Begonias, many of which bloom the year round and come in a variety of sizes, are excellent terrarium plants. Not only are their flower colors lovely, but their hardy leaves are tinged with scarlet, silver-pink, and bronze red! They are almost fool-proof to grow and need filtered sunlight, a rich garden soil and good drainage. Do not overwater them. Especially suited for the terrarium are the miniature varieties, such as the *Begonia-rex cultorum*. The larger types such as the begonia fern with white blossoms and the begonia dancing girl with leaves of silver-pink, scarlet and green can be used, if care is taken to keep them pruned.

Miniature Orchids — One of the reference books I have been using is called *Garden in Your Window* by Jean Hersey. This book, published in 1949, tells how Mrs. Hersey was one of the first to successfully grow orchids under glass as easily as more common house plants. Miniature orchids (which come in a variety of colors) need, in addition to the potting soil, to be kept in their pocket of osmunda or fir bark. They require a bed with good drainage and, once planted, some sphagnum moss around them. Some orchids like sun while others need to be kept cool. The miniature varieties of the *Bulbophyllum* and *Cirrhopetalum* genera do very well in the warm, moist atmosphere of the covered terrarium. They show flower colors of red, pink, dark purple and yellow-brown. Give sun to *Bulbophyllum* and occasional sun to *Cirrhopetalum*.

Wintergreen — It has hardy leaves and crimson berries.

Partridge berry — This plant bears scarlet fruit. (Both it and wintergreen will add color to your woodland terrarium.)

Pilea — These plants are perfect for terrarium growing, as they like filtered sun and high humidity. The *Pilea involucrata* is a creeper that has miniature flowers growing in clusters on the leaves.

Gloxinia — Gloxinias burst forth with a great variety of color. They are usually grown in the greenhouse and thus are perfect for the terrarium. The bell-like flowers may have colored throats as well as bands of color on the petals. Shades of pink, red, blue, purple are common.

Cactus — Many plants in the cactus family put out a colorful flower. The red-head cactus, which has a bright red flower perched on its top is small enough for a desertarium. Also pleasing is the *Cactus notocactus* with its bright yellow flower. But do look around for others that are colorful and suitable for terrarium planting. The variety is virtually limitless.

PLANTS WHOSE LEAVES PROVIDE COLOR

The leaves of certain plants are so variegated and colorful that they provide a gay note to the terrarium much in the way that a flower does. Many plants have leaves whose colors are more varied than those of some flowers! No longer must you think in terms of leaves being only green for they can range from white to deep purple and be as interestingly patterned as they are colorful.

Strawberry geranium — Also known as Mother-of-Thousands, this plant has mature leaves that are pink and scalloped. Runners from the plant base end in a cluster of tiny leaves. They like moisture, full or partial shade, and a cool spot.

Caladium — Caladiums have leaves that are not only fancy in color, but the same leaf may have a variety of tints of one color on it! They are tropical plants that like partial shade and high humidity. If you wish deep colors make the terrarium soil acidy and keep it moist. Their leaves, resembling an arrowhead, have great color variety. Colors are pink, white, bright red, silver and deepest red. Many leaves give a marbled effect.

Pilea — The aluminum plant (*P. cadierei minima*) with silver-green leaves and the light green-leafed artillery plant (*P. microphylla*) both provide interest of color.

Peperomia — The watermelon begonia (*Peperomia sandersi argyreia*) has red leaf-stems with silver-striped leaves. Another form of watermelon begonia, *Peperomia sandersi*, with its silver-veined leaves, also looks and does well in a terrarium.

Peperomias and pileas, as I have mentioned before, are musts for the indoor glass garden. They not only provide leaf color and form, but are low growers that like warmth and high humidity.

Venus's-Flytrap — This interesting colorful plant wants full sun and moisture to simulate its native environment of the savannahs of South Carolina. They grow well in a bed of rich soil covered with sphagnum moss. The leaves are bright green with a deep yellow center. While it is true that the Venus's Flytrap likes to dine upon flies and other insects, should they be in short supply, they take their nourishment from the soil.

Glacier Ivy — *(Hedera Helix* "Glacier"). Small green leaves bordered in white make this ivy unusual. It likes a cool spot either in sun or shade. In the terrarium it has to be kept cut back or it will tend to be sprawling. Keep the soil moist and uncover some of the time.

Coleus — The foliage of these plants has many varieties of shade and color. Its interestingly shaped leaves may be heartlike, oval or frilled. All shades of foliage—green, yellow, red, brown and pink—may be found on the coleus. Use a potting soil to plant them in and keep it moist. For best colors, give coleus some sunlight. Their only two drawbacks are mealy bugs (somewhat eliminated in a terrarium) and the need for careful pruning to keep them small.

Dieffenbachia — This species is also referred to as the mother-in-law plant as it is purported to cause temporary speechlessness if a piece of the stem or leaf is chewed or placed under the tongue! Its mottled green, ivy and yellow leaves are quite goodlooking. Care must be taken that it does not get too large and take over the surrounding plants. Give dieffenbachia warmth and sun for a couple of hours daily.

Chlorophytum elatum — (Spider plant) This interesting-looking South African plant puts out small runners and has light green leaves with white striped centers. It needs horizontal growing room, sun and moisture.

Wandering Jew — Very hardy in the terrarium, the foliage of this plant is a deep red-purple on the underside, with a silvery green topside veined in lighter green. For the most colorful leaves give this plant sun and moist roots.

COLOR FROM TINY TREES

One of the most intriguing ideas to me is planting a tiny tree in a glass house! They not only provide color, but linear interest as well. Seedling trees and dwarf types are fine for terrariums and enhance the woodland landscape with a variety of colors and forms. The height and shape of even the smallest tree will bring a touch of woodsiana to the indoor garden. Search for these trees in the fall woods or order them through the mails or at local nurseries. One word of caution, if you pick your own, be sure that it is in an area where you are allowed to do so. Some places have restrictions as to what you can take with you! If allowed, dig up the tree and its roots with a trowel and keep it moist as you take it home. When you are ready to plant it in the terrarium, find a container that will provide vertical growing room. Just one dwarf tree can stand alone for beauty and interest.

Seedling trees recommended for indoor glass gardens are: firs, spruce, hemlock, common junipers, white and ground pine, young red cedars and yew. Any one of these, alone or with a lower plant for contrast, will bring the north woods into the southern apartment! Colors of red, silver and deep greens and interesting silhouettes will give you peace and tranquility.

COLOR FROM BLOOMS

Robert C. Baur, renowned indoor gardener and popular author of articles in the New York Times and the book

Gardens in Glass Containers, has written much on blossoms of all sorts in the glass garden. I have read many articles of his and find them to be unique and fascinating in their ideas.

Do you know that if you want lily of the valley in your living room, you need not wait for spring? While nature takes a rest outdoors, it need not be so indoors. There are twigs, blossoms and "pips" available to you that can be forced to bloom in antique candy jars or large brandy snifters. An added bonus is the fragrance that will greet you each time you open the top to peek in or give the plants an airing!

What was a dull, lifeless table will become a pinpoint of pleasure with a flowering glass garden on it. Add some green moss and small plants for accent and the picture is complete.

Lily of the valley "pips" — A "pip" is a piece of root with a bud at the top. There are especially prepared lily of the valley "pips" available from dealers that are excellent for forcing. These flowering beauties will provide a dainty touch of white and green to your clear glass container. They can be forced in almost any medium that can be kept moist. Sphagnum moss is fine, as well as sand. Place the roots in the moistened bed with the buds sticking up. Keep them in a dark place for ten days and then give this terrarium partial sun. Cover, but allow for some air and light to avoid mold. Watch the tiny bell-like flowers open and delight.

Violet roots — The lovely deep color and fragrant odor of the violet can be yours under glass. If the plants are not available in your own garden, you may buy them at a local nursery or through the mail. Violet roots should be planted in topsoil that has been placed on a bed of moss. Add some charcoal and gravel. Gently press the roots with the "eyes" out into the soil and water before closing the top. Violets will pop into bloom in about five weeks in a cool spot in the house. Set them in filtered sun only.

Planting twigs — Cut twigs in the garden when the branches are well budded. With pruning shears make a slantwise cut, getting a twig in proportion to the size of the bowl you will use for it. Plant these in aquarium gravel placed in the bottom of your glass container. They bloom much bigger than when planted so take this into consideration when you size the twigs and don't overcrowd. Try twigs of pussy willow, dogwood, cherry, forsythia and weeping willow. Soak for at least 24 hours before planting. Keep twigs in glass bowls in a cool dark area until they start to blossom. When color begins to appear, give them some sun.

Color for the terrarium is possible at all times of the year and in all parts of the country. Leaves and flowers, trees and blossoms all help to set a mood and warm your heart. With a minimum of planning you will be able to have four seasons of colorful plantings for your house, your apartment or your office.

CHAPTER SEVEN: WIDE-TOP AND DOME TERRARIUMS

Whether you have decided to start with a wide-top terrarium (and this is perhaps wisest for beginners) or are going to brave it and plunge right into the bottle, there are guidelines that apply to both. This chapter begins with a discussion of those applicable to all types of terrarium planting and then goes more deeply into planting wide-top containers. Chapter Eight deals with the techniques unique to bottle planting.

First, relax. Look upon this as a fun project—one that will allow you to try many new things artistically as well as technically. You do not have to buy and plant in the same day. Sometimes I find it advantageous to decide on my container, purchase the plants and then live with the raw materials for a few days to get the feel of them. I experiment with placement outside the container and on paper. Mentally I plan how I would like the finished project to look. This gives me a chance to avoid placing a plant where I do not want it and perhaps needing to replant it. However, unless you keep ferns in a very humid atmosphere and well watered, they may dry out before being put into the terrarium. This can be prevented by temporarily inverting a large-mouth glass jar or dome over them.

If you can, take your container when you shop and measure the plants in relation to where they will be placed. Doing this will avoid overbuying for a particular container as the plants can be sized to fit space and shape. Inquire which plants are slow growers and consider these first. Seedling-size plants are a good investment since, if you start out with plants which are too large or even just right, they may outgrow their confines sooner than you would wish. This can happen in a large pickle jar as well as a slender wine decanter! It is similar to planting a shrub outside of a new house. If it is in proportion to the size of the house when you first plant it, you can be sure than in five years it will have grown to look too large, and in ten, gigantic!

Where you work on making your terrarium will, of course, depend on the space accessible to you. Even the drainboard next to the kitchen sink can be a planting area. A potting table is ideal as supplies can be left out and always ready for use. Should space be limited, the floor is fine if you protect it with newspaper that can be rolled up and discarded. Allow for elbow room for you will soon find yourself spreading out everywhere! Should it be necessary for you to pack all your paraphernalia away after each use, then simply keep a carton for that purpose and store it in a closet or the garage.

Before beginning any planting, take care to see that your container is scrupulously clean. A sparkling glass will show off your plants to far better advantage than one coated with even the finest film of dust. I use the dishwasher for those that will fit. Others can be soaked for a time in a solution of laundry bleach, plain soap and water or window spray. It is best to let the container air for at least 24 hours after cleaning to avoid exposing the plants to fumes from ammonia or other cleaning agents.

The two secrets of success in any terrarium are a porous, flaky soil and proper drainage. If your initial watering is done correctly, and the soil does not become too wet, then roots will receive adequate air and water. Care must be taken in all terrariums not to overwater at the outset, particularly if you are using a watertight container as there is no way for run-off to occur.

Make the soil bed 1/4 of the height of the container. Thus, if you are using a 12" water jug, your soil level would be three inches. This can vary somewhat if the container is odd-shaped or very narrow.

SUGGESTED ORDER FOR PLANTING THE TERRARIUM

(1) Plant largest specimens.
(2) Add smaller plants.
(3) Trailing plants are put in.
(4) Ground covers are placed in empty spaces.
(5) Gravel or redwood chips placed where needed.
(6) Small accessories added, if desired.

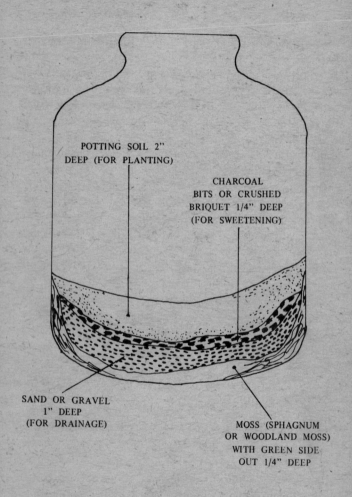

POTTING SOIL 2"
DEEP (FOR PLANTING)

CHARCOAL
BITS OR CRUSHED
BRIQUET 1/4" DEEP
(FOR SWEETENING)

SAND OR GRAVEL
1" DEEP
(FOR DRAINAGE)

MOSS (SPHAGNUM
OR WOODLAND MOSS)
WITH GREEN SIDE
OUT 1/4" DEEP

Figure 7.
Diagram of the layers in a Terrarium
(Inches are approximate for a 12" container)

RULES OF GREEN THUMB FOR TERRARIUM-MAKING

(1) Relax and enjoy yourself.

(2) Consider the overall effect you desire. Each plant should blend into the setting. Will it look right and pleasing to the eye?

(3) Scale your plants to the scene. If a woodland scene, scale them according to how they are in nature. How will you reproduce it?

(4) Do not crowd plants. Give them growing and breathing room. Open spots can be covered with moss.

(5) Consider a primary center of interest and then secondary ones.

(6) Plan a center path that will pull your eye deeper into the scene.

(7) If the container is to be viewed from one side only, place the taller plants in the back. Then plant smaller ones up front.

(8) Always face plants front in a container that is to be viewed from only one side.

(9) If the container is to be viewed in the round, place tall plants in the center with smaller ones around them.

(10) Mound the soil. Hilly terrains are more interesting than flat ones.

(11) Terrariums that are to be viewed from one side should be fullest in back and then built down to the front. Cover stems of taller plants with lower-growing plants placed in front of them.

(12) Place light leaves next to dark leaves.

(13) Plant thick-leafed plants next to thin-leafed ones.

(14) If the leaves of one plant are sharp, plant a rounded-leaf plant next to it.

(15) Textured leaves and nontextured leaves set each other off when they are placed adjacently.

(16) Use plants that have a variety of growing habits. Put low-growers next to vertical ones.

(17) Size them in proportion to one another and to the container.

(18) Set newly-planted terrariums in shade for a week before giving any sun.

(19) The more soil you are able to leave on the roots in planting, the less shock to the plant.

(20) Stand back and delight in the fruits of your labor!

MAKING THE DOME-TOP TERRARIUM

Jack Kramer in his book, *Gardens Under Glass*, introduced me to the possibility of the dome-top terrarium. Since reading it, I have seen numerous plants under domes as well as empty glass domes for sale. A recent department store advertisement brought news of a terrarium kit. It consists of a plastic, elliptical dome with a small hole in the top for air. It comes complete with soil and gravel, and is available in three sizes.

Dome-top terrariums are extremely easy to plant as the placing of the plants is done before the top ever goes on. It is essentially like making a dish garden and then placing a top on it! These terrariums are lovely to look at. Their graceful vertical line offsets perfectly even one tall branching plant. They make for easy care and can be added to or trimmed with minimum effort.

To make a dome terrarium you will need:

(1) A bottom receptacle for the soil and plants. A deep dish or planting tray serves this purpose well. Drainage holes are an advantage.

(2) A dome for the top. This may be a plastic cake cover or clear glass or plastic dome. Very suitable for this purpose are the glass domes sometimes seen over wax fruit or stuffed birds. You can fit the top to the bottom or the bottom to the top, as long as there is no air space.

(3) Planting medium, the plants and decorative items.

Steps in planting a woodland dome:

(1) Obtain mosses and small plants from the woods, mail-order houses or nurseries.

(2) Prepare the planting bed in a bowl and plant.

(3) Water lightly and cover with dome.

(4) Place out of direct sunlight.

(5) Rotate occasionally so that plants do not tilt toward the light.

One of the delights in this dome terrarium is that the moss will sprout and new woodland surprises will appear almost immediately.

PLANTING THE AQUARIUM CASE

For ease of planting and growing room for your plants, a square or rectangular aquarium container is perfect. The large opening allows both hands to move about freely inside for placing the plants and decorations. If you object to the wooden or metal strips that hold the glass together at the corners, a terrarium case is now sold made from flat sheets of transparent acrylic plastic, cemented at the corners with epoxy resin. They may be bought in a variety of sizes and include covers and crushed glass for drainage. Basically the same shape as aquarium cases, they are expedient to plant. Smaller drum-shaped aquariums may also be planted, but more dexterity and patience are needed due to the smaller top openings.

Another possibility in planting the aquarium case is to leave the plants in their pots and place them pot and all in the case. This will limit their growth and enable you to move them about or thin them without disturbing the entire scene. This, as was mentioned previously, is an excellent place to keep plants that are in need of revival.

To make a tropical aquarium terrarium you will need:
1. An aquarium. (One with a slight leak, no longer good for fish, can be used.)
2. Soil and drainage material.
3. Plants such as philodendron, ivy, ferns, Chinese evergreens, African violets. You can pick and choose any that please you and live well together under tropical conditions.
4. Finishing touches—moss, bark or other decorations.

Steps in planting a tropical aquarium case:
1. Place drainage material on bottom.
2. Prepare the soil bed in proportion to the height of the container. Remember that a hilly terrain is more interesting; so mound your earth at the ends of the case.

3. Place the larger plants at either end of the case.
4. Fill in with smaller plants as you progress toward the center.
5. Add ground cover (moss, Baby's Tears, low-growing plants, etc.) and other decorative touches.
6. Water the soil and plants lightly till moist.
7. Cover with lid leaving air space or prop the top up with a wood sliver. (Some air is necessary to avoid rot and mildew in this tropical case.) If no top is available, a cellophane wrap cover with several holes in it can be used. Because of accumulating moisture, this case will have a natural jungle look.

ABOUT BUBBLES AND BRANDY SNIFTERS

The principles involved in planting the bubble and the brandy snifter are essentially the same. Both containers allow the plants inside to be viewed in the round, or a front can be decided on and planting done accordingly.

Bubbles are just that—a glass bubble with an opening on the top. Brandy snifters are somewhat more tapered and stand on their own glass pedestal. For both, assemble the same basic materials as are needed for the aquarium or dome planter.

A bubble is measured at its widest part around and its size should determine the number of plants you will place in it. Brandy snifters are measured by their capacity in ounces and, here too, the size determines the density of planting. If you plant attractively and sparsely, the plants in both will fill out and enhance the containers.

Size of Bubble	Suggested Number of Plants of 2-1/4" Pot Size
8"	5
10"	7 (4 tall, 3 short)
12"	10
14"	12
16"	12 or more (3" pot-size plants may be used here.)

Size of Brandy Snifter	Suggested Number of Plants of 2-1/4" Pot Size
160 ounces	5
256 ounces	7
414 ounces	9
820 ounces	12 (3" pot size may be used here.)

Steps in planting an 8" bubble terrarium (numbered on side view):

1. Put in layer of charcoal or gravel for drainage.
2. Mound the dirt in the back so as to resemble a hill.
3. Place moss liner on sides of glass.
4. Poke five holes in soil where plants are to go.
5. Gently remove tallest plant from pot by tapping on table edge.
6. Plant tallest plant in rear center, facing front. (Facing plants front will allow them to cover their own stems.)

7. Place the four other plants with their tallest leaves towards side of the bubble.
8. Leave a small path down the center for growth and/or decoration.
9. Water with sprayer till soil is moist. This will also pack it down.
10. Wipe any soil from sides of bubble with damp cloth and brush earth from plant leaves with soft paint brush.
11. Cover.

DESERTARIUMS

Cacti and succulents require much drier conditions than most other plants. Since both need a sandy soil, some sun and little water, they may be planted together in the desert terrarium (or desertarium). Put them in a glass case with a wide-top opening and leave uncovered to allow for maximum air circulation. Minimal care is needed for these slow-growing and durable plants. Pack them in tightly, as their roots require little room. With the addition of wooden cubes painted to resemble desert dwellings, a miniature scene can be created on your windowsill.

Suggested plants for the desertarium are:

Cacti—choose from many varieties
Opuntia
Kalanchoes
Echeverias
Crassulas
Aloes

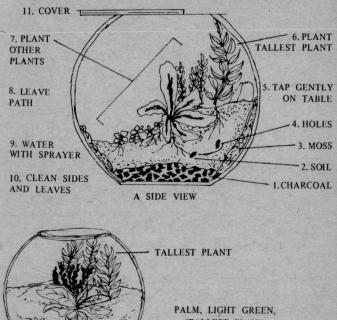

11. COVER

7. PLANT OTHER PLANTS

8. LEAVE PATH

9. WATER WITH SPRAYER

10. CLEAN SIDES AND LEAVES

6. PLANT TALLEST PLANT

5. TAP GENTLY ON TABLE

4. HOLES

3. MOSS

2. SOIL

1. CHARCOAL

A SIDE VIEW

TALLEST PLANT

A FRONT VIEW

PALM, LIGHT GREEN, (TALLEST PLANT)

VICTORIA FERN, WHITE AND GREEN

BIRD'S NEST FERN, LIGHT GREEN

STRAWBERRY, DARK GREEN AND RED

HEART IVY, GREEN AND DARK GREEN

A TOP VIEW

Figure 8.
Suggested Layout for Bubble Planting

Sedums
Cotyledons
Agaves
Sansevierias

FINISHING TOUCHES

When you stand back and admire your planted terrarium, you may decide it is complete as is or you may wish to add some finishing touches. Care should be taken, however, to avoid clutter, or nothing will stand out and everything will be a jumbled mess! The type of terrarium should dictate what you will add as a decorative touch. In the woodland scene it is best to have rocks, stones, twigs, branches or bark. An unusual small stone or well-placed lichen-covered rock can become a center of interest but should not detract from the plants themselves.

If you cannot resist small ceramic animals (I can!), choose them with discretion and even then—only one small reindeer, elf or frog per terrarium—please! These can be placed in the soil on a small piece of toothpick. Very large figurines are inappropriate and gaudily colored ones will only detract from the whole. In choosing a nongrowing item for the terrarium, it is best to ask yourself, "Will it really add to my enjoyment of the scene?"

Making a terrarium brings out the creative artist in all of us. Following rules of good design will result in a polished finished product. True, there are space limits in a terrarium, but all the more of a challenge! Care in placing of your plants will result in a well-balanced composite of nature. With a minimum of practice and patience you will be able to accomplish the look you like.

CHAPTER EIGHT: PLANTING THE NARROW-NECK CONTAINER

I know a woman who does the most whimsical and creative needlework! Each time I meet her she has created something new, exciting and different. With admiration for her talent, I questioned her as to where she gets her ideas and know-how. Her answer was, "I am not afraid to try anything. You see only the successes. Many times things do not work, but I try and I learn and more often than not I succeed." It occurs to me that this is an excellent way of approaching the making of a bottle garden. Know-how and patience are necessary, but also a spirit of adventure-in-creating, such as my friend so obviously has!

Come to the narrow-neck bottle with gentleness. Forcing a plant roughly through the opening and quickly down into the soil will seldom work. These bottles do require skill and special tools, but they are a worthwhile challenge to any indoor gardener. Once you have secured your first plant in the soil, you will realize it is easier than it looks!

PLANTS FOR NARROW-NECK CONTAINERS

When selecting plants to go in the narrow-neck bottle, remember that the very shape of the bottle will give it an almost constant moist atmosphere. Buy plants that like moisture and are partial to shade. Avoid plants that do not do well in a closed-top container. Since the leaves and the stem have to be pushed through the skinny passageway of the neck, decide on plants with *strong* leaves and stems. You will find it difficult to pass a very thin, fragile-stem plant through the narrow neck. In general small, low plants have sturdy leaves and stems. I have also found that if a plant is top-heavy, it is hard to balance it correctly in the soil. In a bottle, as in other containers, plant together those specimens with similar requirements. Learn the plant's growth habits and consider if it will conform well with the silhouette of the bottle.

Plants suggested for the bottle garden are:

Baby's Tears
Strawberry begonia
Chinese evergreen
Dwarf palm
Grape ivy
Prayer plant
Peperomia
Ferns and mosses
Umbrella sedge

PREPARATORY STEPS

If you take the time to set up all the supplies you will need for your bottle garden before beginning, you will save time and effort later on. Try holding a plant upright in the soil while you search around for a tamping tool and you will soon find out why this is necessary!

Suggested steps:

1. Gather materials—tools, supplies, washed and dried bottles and plants.

2. Set up your work area on a potting bench, or on a table top covered with paper or plastic.

3. Choose plants that will provide contrast in color, size, leaf pattern and texture.

4. Try the arrangement of the plants outside of the bottle. Also, size them next to it. Move them around until you are pleased with the arrangement. This will give you a good basis for placing them in the soil. You can also outline the bottom of the bottle on paper and sketch-plant on that.

5. Remove all dead and yellowed leaves and prune questionable ones. This is much easier to do outside of the bottle.

6. Prepare the planting "bed" as follows:

   a. Place a bed of woodland moss (green side out) or damp sphagnum moss (which has been wet and then squeeze-dried) in the bottom of the bottle. This can be done with a wooden dowel. Shape it into a cup! The height of your bottle should determine the height of the moss cup—approximately one-fourth the height of your container.

b. Place your funnel over the cardboard tube on the neck of the bottle and pour the drainage material (gravel or rock) through it. If your bottle has drainage holes on the bottom (you can have holes drilled in the bottom by a glass cutter), add only half as much gravel as you would for nonholed bottoms. Spread the drainage material evenly on top of the moss cup.

c. Pour in small pieces of charcoal for sweetening.

d. Pour the soil through the funnel to the bottom. Soil should be damp to the touch but not too wet or it will not pour freely. Soil level should be to the top of the moss cup. Jiggle bottle to even out soil layer.

e. Poke holes in the soil with your dowel where the plants are to go.

f. Remove plants from pots by gently tapping on table edge.

g. Gently wash roots free of soil and inspect them with a magnifying glass for insects and health. Remove any insects.

h. Trim the root if it is too long for the depth of the planting bed or too wide to pass through the neck opening.

Before lowering the plants into the bottle, decide which will be the front. Then, for a uniform design, face all plants front. Put the tallest one in first, in the middle of the bottle, as it will need the most vertical growing room. Next plant the smaller ones and finally the low growers and ground cover. This placement makes for symmetry with the tallest in the background and the miniatures and sprawlers in the foreground.

The numbers and sizes of the plants you select should be determined by the size and the shape of the bottle. Fewer well-placed ones will be far more effective than a jumbled mess of stems and leaves.

STEPS IN PLANTING

1. Set the plant's roots in the placer with the top resting on top of the prongs.
2. Carefully ease the plant, roots first, into the neck of the bottle, compacting the leaves with your hand, if necessary. Ease plant through neck of bottle.
3. Place the plant in the hole you have dug for it, taking care not to mash the roots or place them or the leaves against the sides of the glass.
4. Secure the roots in the soil by covering them with at least 1/2-inch of soil and packing firmly with your tamping tool. (I find this is easier to do if placer is still lightly holding plant.) Roots that are difficult to secure may be anchored with a small stone or pebble. If a plant is top-heavy, give it added support by putting a smaller plant at its base.
5. Remove tools through neck after plant is secure.

In making the bottle garden you will be working with exposed or nearly exposed roots. Special care should be taken not to damage them. Allow ample room in the soil and never crowd them. When placing soil around exposed roots, be exceptionally gentle as you tamp over and between them.

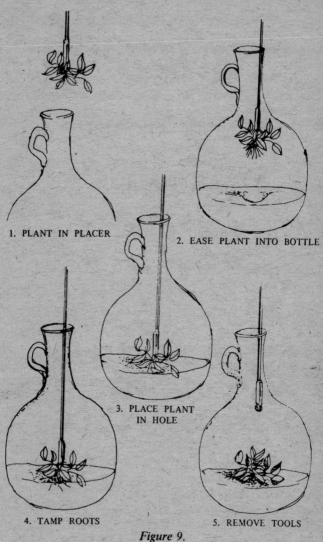

1. PLANT IN PLACER

2. EASE PLANT INTO BOTTLE

3. PLACE PLANT
IN HOLE

4. TAMP ROOTS

5. REMOVE TOOLS

Figure 9.
Steps in planting narrow-neck containers

FINISHING TOUCHES

Any added attraction must naturally be small enough to pass through the neck of the container. A more finished look will be achieved by covering the soil with colored aquarium gravel or patches of moss. Natural touches, such as tiny pebbles and pieces of wood, will not detract from the desired feel of the bottle garden.

As careful as you may be, there will probably be excess dirt and moss on the sides of the bottle. Use a curved bottle brush or cotton swab that has been tied to a dowel to remove it. Clean the outside with a soft damp cloth.

The initial watering is a crucial factor in the further well-being of the bottle garden. Some thought must be given to the type of plants you are using. There is no one right way to water the completed garden and each expert in the field seems to have his own particular procedure.

Different ways in which initial watering may be done:

1. Pour 1/2 cup of room temperature water through a funnel to the bottom of the bottle.
2. Sprinkle the plants and the soil with a spray bottle until they are fairly moist.
3. Pour water in through the funnel until the water level reaches the top of the drainage material.

You may cork the bottle or cover in another way. If you wish, put a few holes in the cork to allow for air. Many people do not cork bottle gardens at all, as there is little room for moisture to escape through the narrow-neck opening. Corking the bottle will prevent evaporation, but may lead to the problem of mold or rot. You can tell if there is a correct amount of moisture present in the terrarium by the amount of condensation on the sides of the bottle. If heavy water drops occur, you will have to dry the bottle out by removing its top (if there is one) for a day or so. Another way to dry out the soil quickly is by means of a portable hair dryer. But do go easy if you try this method! If the soil is too dry after a few days, water lightly again. To be in perfect balance, a light water vapor should occur only at night, when the outside temperature drops. The moisture will drip back onto the plants and your bottle garden will be self-sustaining.

Place the finished garden out of direct sunlight and away from high temperatures. Occasionally, it will require pruning, cutting back and cleaning. More vigorous plants may have to be removed entirely. It is probably wise not to feed the bottle garden, as feeding will encourage too rapid growth.

CHAPTER NINE:
CARE OF
THE TERRARIUM

Although they are relatively care-free, there is a certain amount of tender and loving attention which you will have to give your terrarium. With basic care, knowledge and interest, you can expect lasting enjoyment from your creation. The high level of humidity maintained in a terrarium makes it practically self-sufficient, but not entirely. However the amount of time devoted to caring for your glass garden will be minute when compared with the hours of pleasure it will afford you. Even completely covered cases need a watchful eye to make sure they are flourishing. Plants may yellow, leaves die or mold form. Pay attention and observe your terrarium. It will tell you what it needs!

If you have been conscientious in assembling the materials,

have taken care to provide the right environment for woodland and jungle plants, and have provided slightly different conditions for the cacti and succulents, then maintenance will be a simple task. If you have chosen slow-growing plants, and arranged those together that need the same growing conditions, a major part of the care is already under way.

With today's renewed interest in greenery for the home, there is no limit to the facts and figures available to help you in your task. Nurseries put out pamphlets on the making and care of terrariums. Plant shopkeepers no longer let you just walk out with a plant. They tell you all about it so you can take over at home where they have left off. Indoor-Garden tool kits are sold which include many of the implements needed to care for the terrarium. Once you have made one you have a responsibility to look after it. The only two limiting factors are insufficient knowledge and lack of interest. In our ecological and green-minded world, these can be virtually eliminated. The question of watering, airing, lighting, trimming and pest control will concern you. You have created a living thing and you cannot abandon it just as it is starting out.

WATERING THE TERRARIUM

Opinions differ on watering of the terrarium. Several factors can and will influence the schedule. For me to claim that yours will require no watering, or watering once a week or every other week would be foolish. Only you, who will be watching it every day, can know if, and when, it should be watered. The literature contains varying opinions and controversy goes on about the need for watering at all. Some experts, as I have previously mentioned, keep tight covers on their cases and never water. Others advise no cover and a more rigorous watering plan. Each is right, but only for himself. You will have to determine how you can keep the correct balance of moisture in your terrarium. In terrariums that do not have drainage holes (and many do not), watering must be done with extreme care to avoid soil saturation.

Varying advice on watering by experts includes:
1. Water at an interval of ten days.
2. Give your terrarium one or two teaspoons of water once a month.
3. Your terrarium will not ever require watering if the bottle opening is small.
4. Water covered terrariums every eighteen months and uncovered terrariums every six months.
5. Give one-third of a cup of water when the soil is slightly dry in appearance.
6. Water the bottle garden when evaporation moisture and condensation no longer recycle.
7. Normal watering interval ranges from 2 to 3 months—when condensation no longer is seen on the inside of the container or droplets on the leaves.
8. With terrariums with tightly fitting lids, a number of weeks may go by before they need any attention.

Guidelines

There are certain factors that can act as guidelines in establishing a watering plan for your terrarium. Taking these facts into consideration, you water only when your plants need it and not on any set time schedule. The watering of your terrarium will depend on these factors:

1. The amount of initial watering given.
2. The kinds of plants in the case. For example, cacti, which lose water very slowly, need a less frequent watering schedule than thin-leafed plants.
3. The temperature of the room.
4. The size of the top opening.
5. If the case is at least partially open, the amount of humidity in the air.

Things to look for

Factors that will help you to determine when to water your terrarium:

1. Water woodland or jungle terrariums immediately after planting. Withhold water from the desertarium for a few days to allow for healing of the delicate root system, which may have been injured in transplanting.
2. Dig the soil with a spoon (in wide-top terrariums) or with a glass straw (in narrow tops) to see if it is moist to the touch.
3. If bowl is exceptionally light when picked up, it may indicate lack of soil moisture.
4. If the soil is lighter in color than usual it may need water.
5. Tap the bottom of the bowl. If a ringing sound is produced, it could indicate a need for watering.
6. Water with room temperature water when bottom layer of soil no longer feels moist.
7. A crisp appearance to moss indicates a need for water.
8. Check the condensation on the glass. If it no longer appears even at night, water is needed.

AIRING THE TERRARIUM

Ventilating the terrarium is a necessity. Very few plants can survive in the 100 percent humidity of the constantly closed case. Without air, too much water would condense on the glass and completely obscure the plants from view. Fresh air is also needed to keep this enclosure sweet smelling. Exchange of air when the top is opened will cause stale moist air to leave the terrarium and fresh dry air to enter it. This is necessary to prevent the decay and rot which can result from constantly covered cases. Although it may necessitate more frequent watering, some fresh air is a must. You will know when the top should be left off by:

1. Accumulation of excessive moisture on the glass.
2. Water standing on the bottom of the case.
3. Appearance of rot or fungus damage.
4. Signs of mold or mildew.

How long and how often to remove the cover, only you can ascertain. Here again, as with watering, the plants involved, the dryness in the surrounding air, the recycling moisture, the tightness of the cover—all will help guide you. If removing the cover at regular intervals—say once every week for 24 hours—keeps your terrarium in balance, then do it. Perhaps you will have to have it uncovered more or less than that. How you cover and air your plants under glass will be determined by the atmosphere of your home and the warning signals the terrarium itself will give you.

LIGHT AND TEMPERATURE

Along with fresh air and watering needs, you must also consider the light and temperature requirements of the terrarium. It needs either indirect sun or artificial light. Except for flowering plants and some desertariums, direct sunlight should be avoided. Clear glass acts as a heat magnifier and if sun were to beat on it, the intense rays would cause leaf burn and kill the plants.

A woodland case will require less direct light than will a desertarium. Give cacti and succulents as much light as possible. Keeping newly made terrariums in a shady place until they take root is recommended. Turning the terrarium will avoid plants leaning toward the light. If artificial light is used, have it on the plants for at least twelve hours a day.

One of the advantages of the terrarium is that plants inside it are insulated against quick shifts in air temperature. However, try to keep the temperature in your room as even as possible. For bottle gardens 70° with a slight drop at night is fine. Woodland terrariums can stand a cooler temperature than can a desertarium. Naturally temperature changes can not be eliminated completely. Sometimes a quick shift will be evidenced by clouding of the glass. Experiment with placing your terrarium in different locations to see where the light and temperature conditions are best for it.

TRIMMING AND REPLACING

A time will come when you will have to trim, prune and perhaps even replant a terrarium. The plants that went in small can sometimes outgrow their enclosure. Be ruthless in trimming! As difficult as it may be for you to bring yourself to cut or snip a leaf—or remove a plant entirely—it must be done for the good health and appearance of the arrangement. Try not to become so attached to any plant that removing it will be an impossible job. If a plant is yellowing and dying, remove it completely and add one that will not detract.

Prune dead leaves with regularity. Shape the plant to conform to the contours of the glass. Break off unwanted shoots and overly vigorous growth. In the wide-top case this can be done by snipping off the leaves with your fingers. In bottle gardens, use a pruning tool. Remove the plants that are too big for the case and replant with smaller ones or none at all. Care should be taken to leave, undisturbed, plants or parts of plants that you do not care to remove. If you have started plants from seeds, weed out the weaker ones to encourage survival of the strongest.

Before any trimming, however, note what it is that's happening and try to figure out why. Ferns go through a seasonal drying out process which is natural and dry leaves may not be a sign that they are dead. Yellowing foliage caused by too much sun may be able to recover if you take the plant out of the sunlight or give it more ventilation. Feeding the plant may also help overcome yellowing. Brown leaves are caused when the plants touch the glass, wet with condensation. This can be overcome by keeping the condensation at a lower level.

The possibility of removing a plant entirely and trimming it and then replanting has already been discussed. This is a delicate task and should be undertaken with the utmost care. Terrarium cases no longer aesthetically pleasing may be replanted entirely by removing all the plants and soil carefully and starting over again.

FEEDING THE TERRARIUM

Feeding the plants in your terrarium can be a rather touchy proposition. You do not want to fertilize them so well that they will burst their confines. However, if you have had a terrarium for a number of years, you will have to provide it with some nourishment. If you take care to watch the daily progress and no problems are cropping up, then a feeding every six months will probably be adequate.

Terrariums can be fed with any good all-purpose balanced fertilizer. Dilute the fertilizer with twice as much water as is directed for regular house plants. Add the liquid to the soil by means of a baster or funnel, taking care not to get any of it on the greens of the plants.

ADVERSE FACTORS THAT CAN AFFECT THE TERRARIUM

By the very nature of a terrarium—a small controlled environment—pests will be at a minimum. Using a sterilized commercial brand soil also lessens the danger of unwanted organisms. An excess of condensation can cause mold or mildew to form on the plants. None of these factors should be beyond your control, except perhaps for the red spider, and then it is best to burn the plant and start again!

Problems That May Occur	Prevention	Treatment
1. Mildew	Airing the case at intervals	Remove top after taking off mildewed parts
2. Mold or plant decay	Proper airing	Increased ventilation

3. Aphids	Sterile soil—insecticide spray	Remove with damp cotton swab or blow tobacco smoke into the case and cover it
4. Snails	Sterile soil	Remove with damp swab
5. Mealy bugs	Wash leaves with water or insecticide spray	Insecticide spray
6. Scale insects	Wash leaves etc. (as above)	Insecticide spray
7. White flies	Wash leaves etc. (as above)	Insecticide spray
8. Plant lice	Water or insecticide leaf spray	Spray

Terrariums, like all other living things, need looking after. As is always the case, the more tender and loving the care, the greater the reward. Be kind and gentle, use your knowledge and common sense and your tiny green houses will thrive beautifully.

CHAPTER TEN: TERRARIUMS FOR PEOPLE OF ALL AGES

Terrariums have an appeal for all age groups. Gardening under glass offers unlimited possibilities for enjoyment to both children and adults. Teachers are questioning plant shop owners about the materials and tools necessary to start projects in their classrooms. (Our six-year-old son's class has made a large tropical aquarium case.) Hospitals are learning of the tremendous therapeutic advantages that creating and caring for a growing thing has for shut-ins and convalescents. It is also, interestingly enough, one of the few projects which can be indulged in by people of both sexes without any thought of its being specifically for one or the other! I have seen muscular, bearded men making terrariums as well as petite eight-year-old Brownie Scouts!

Thousands of today's senior citizens have taken to mobile home living. Because there is a smaller amount of land to tend, many have turned to indoor gardening as a way to continue to cultivate their green thumbs. Terrariums can give a trailer that extra special touch of warmth and the personal touch of the person who cares for plants.

Everyone enjoys doing something that is simple, effective and once done, easy to care for. Terrariums meet these requirements. Making them is truly a project for all seasons and for people of all ages.

CHILDREN AND TERRARIUM-MAKING

Planting and children are a winning combination. Terrarium-making is particularly fulfilling to a child, because it allows him to exercise his natural freedom of expression and design. It is refreshing to watch a child involved in the task of gardening in a glass bowl. He instinctively knows what goes where and the effect that pleases him. Rarely will a child need an adult to tell him where to place a plant! He goes about his task with definiteness of purpose and knows exactly when it is finished. Earth, plants and a wide-top glass container are all that is needed to get him on his way. Once finished, his terrarium will be a source of infinite pride and pleasure. It is portable enough to be placed in his own room; so he can observe its progress daily.

My first bottle gardens were made alongside my ten-year-old son who did his in about half the time it took me. The only problem we encountered in doing this project together was that he needed the exact tool I was using the very minute I picked it up. This can be avoided by having two of everything! Better yet, if the child is old enough, encourage him to fashion his own tools and use them. He may surprise you by coming up with something entirely new and inventive.

GETTING THE CHILD SET UP TO WORK

It has been my experience from working with children and watching others do so, that if certain basic steps are taken beforehand, the project will progress much more smoothly. When there are ten exuberant Cub Scouts clamouring about you, anything that will expedite the task is well worth the time and effort. Give the children the responsibility of doing as much setting up as possible. Too, if care has been taken to work in a neat arrangement, cleanup will be easier for you and them.

Steps in setting up a terrarium-making project for children:

1. Decide on a work area where the youngsters will have room to spread out equipment and move with ease. (A play table, a work bench, the floor.)
2. Cover the area with newspaper or plastic to keep it clean.
3. Place the materials needed within reaching distance of each child. If it is not possible to have every tool for each child, talk about the manner in which they can be shared. (This saves arguments later on!)

Essentials include: The plants, soil, gravel, charcoal, dull scissors, planting stick, watering bulb, glass containers, whisk broom (for easy piling of excess dirt), and several damp towels for hand cleaning.

A tool belt to keep equipment in can be made from an old belt and a 6"x 8" brown envelope. Put in it: scissors, planting tools, clipper, etc. The child can wear it while working.

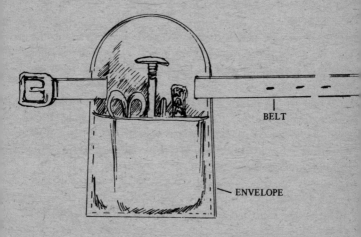

Figure 10.   A Child's Tool Belt

WHAT CHILDREN CAN PLANT

Provide children with plants which assure a high degree of success. Hardy green specimens are excellent. Select those that can withstand rough and tumble handling, for children do get carried away! Arrange for them to use plants with sturdy stems and leaves. Examples of plants for children's terrariums:

Ivy
Wintergreen
Tiny evergreen

Strawberry geranium
Pilea
Peperomia
Ferns—not ultra-delicate kinds

Children enjoy watching things sprout. Seeds planted in a glass jar will yield a variety of surprise growths. Let the child choose grapefruit or orange seeds as well as grass seed and bits of moss.

Plants in the cactus family are fine for children's terrariums. They are sturdy things and can withstand lots of handling. Because cacti are best in a wide-top glass bowl, they will be easy for the child to plant. Examples of cacti for the child's desertarium are:

Zebra haworthia
Old man cactus
Powder puff cactus
Indian head cactus
Sand dollar cactus

VIVARIUMS

Add a small animal or some bugs to a terrarium and give it a whole new life! Vivariums, as they are called, are an attractive way for the child to observe his pets while they go about their daily chores. Here is a firsthand illustration of natural history in his own bedroom! As interesting as a terrarium can be, the including of a live organism in it will make it that much more fascinating to children of all ages. They delight in wee animals and bugs and, with a little knowledge of natural habitat, the child can add his own favorites to the case as he wishes. What fun to watch a living creature move among the marantas or glide up and down the succulents. Animals and bugs, once adjusted to their new home, will allow us humans to look in on them unperturbed while they go about their day-to-day living.

When making a vivarium, the child must take care to place only plants and animals that are compatible together. Desert lizards need cacti and toads like woodland plants; so don't ask them to live under one roof. A fine case for the vivarium is the rectangular aquarium. It allows for ample planting room and there is still space left over for the animals to move about in. Have the child plant the case as he would a terrarium and cover it to keep the animals in. It cannot, however, be airtight.

Provision to feed the animals must be made. Pet shops sell food and have information on the feeding preferences of the small animals of the vivarium.

Creatures	Plants for the Vivarium	Other Facts
1. Lizards (thick-skinned) Geckos (thick-skinned	Desert cacti and succulents	Give them sun and warmth.
2. Snails	Woodland Varieties	These woodland creatures like moist cool conditions (50° temperature).

		They need roaming room and a soil of sand and humus.
Chameleons	Woodland Varieties	Chameleon courtship is fun to watch. The male turns a brilliant emerald when excited!
Turtles	Woodland Varieties	Turtles eat boisterously. Provide them with lettuce so other plants won't be demolished.
Salamanders	Woodland Varieties	
Toads	Woodland Varieties	
3. Bugs	Most types	Can be kept in small spaces. Their work habits are interesting to watch.

If food and drink are provided for the pets in your child's vivarium, they will behave and flourish as they would in their native surroundings. After all, you are providing them with all the comforts of home and they need not go very far afield to find them!

No age or sex barriers exist in terrarium-making. Children as well as adults can design, construct and care for them. They can be made as gifts of love for relatives and friends. Making a glass garden is one activity that allows everyone to work at his own pace and create with as much simplicity or complexity as he feels most comfortable with.

CHAPTER ELEVEN: DECORATING WITH TERRARIUMS

The decorating scheme of any room will be enhanced by the addition of a terrarium. . . or two or three! Glass gardens complement all modes of furnishings.

If modern lines and primary colors are your bent, there is a terrarium for your living room table that will carry out the feel of the scene. For a complete contrast, use plants in an antique decanter! Lend an unexpected note to a colonial den with a tropical terrarium. A woodland terrarium, with its forest of decorative fancy ferns, can be in a room with knotty pine paneling as well as one furnished with oriental antiques. Try terrariums in various spots and see how they look. The tropical jungle aquarium case may be as ideal for the beach hideaway as it is for a plushly-furnished three room office suite. (For an authentic look, construct or buy colorful wooden beasts—giraffes, zebras—and let their tropical browns, tans, and blacks provide still another decorative touch as they "live" among the grape ivy and haworthia.)

Hang a bubble from the ceiling of a covered patio or set one on the kitchen counter to keep you company while you fix the family meals. Treat yourself to a morning pickup by putting a bottle garden in the bathroom. Place a large water jug with ferns and mosses on the floor of an empty room and fill it with gaiety. Greenery as part of the scenery will raise your spirits and perk up a dark corner. Terrariums lend a delightful and decorative touch to your environment. Give thought to the size and shape of the container and the plants inside when placing it. Would they be shown to best advantage on a hallway table or a bookcase in your library? Appropriately situated, a terrarium is a focal point of viewing pleasure.

When you walk into a well-decorated room you know it immediately. Your eye is met with an overall effect of harmony. Only after you have been in it for some time do you begin to identify the little touches that are blended together to create the total look. Some of those touches may well be terrariums! And like the room itself, the terrarium should reveal its separate delights as you inspect it in greater detail.

PLACEMENT OF THE TERRARIUM

Where to place a terrarium in a room is up to you! There are many possibilities and you will discover others for your particular surroundings.

Suggested places for terrariums are:

1. *As centerpieces* Use one large glass bubble in the middle of the dining room table for that special dinner party! (Line the bowl with green moss if you are using your best china and silver.)
   Group planted decanters and wine bottles together on an informal brunch buffet.
   Place one African violet under a dome for a breakfast table eye-opener.
2. *On a table top* Set a brandy snifter garden on a square end table for linear contrast.
   Plant three tall, thin bottles and group them on a small round accent table.
   Give an outdoor feel to an indoor night table with a greenhouse of miniature begonias.
3. *On the floor* Stand a planted water jug in the entry way to your home to greet people.
   Place a large jar-terrarium next to a magazine stand for an island of beauty.
   Place a tropical jug alongside the bathtub for an unexpected touch of nature.

LOOK AROUND

All manner of table, shelf, counter and window ledge will be brightened by the introduction of plantings under glass—herb gardens on the kitchen sill as well as peperomia in the parlor! There are even specially constructed terrarium stands to accommodate a large horizontally planted water jug.

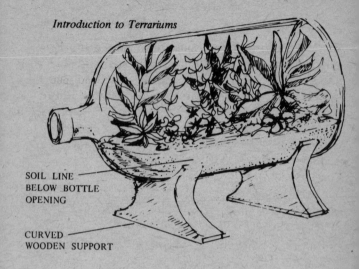

SOIL LINE
BELOW BOTTLE
OPENING

CURVED
WOODEN SUPPORT

Figure 11. A Terrarium Stand

NEW DIRECTIONS

The direction which decorating with terrariums is taking was illustrated by a recent article that appeared in a New York newspaper. It told of the "Aqua Dome," which is actually a round terrarium coffee table. Measuring 40" in diameter and 18" high, it has a glass top covering a large planted clear acrylic bowl on a chrome steel base.

GO CREATIVE—YOU'LL LIKE IT!

Green plants have form and design. Leaves are interesting in their symmetry and shape. Flowering plants have color and fragrance. Both take on a fresh new appeal under glass. Terrariums are easy to make and fun to care for; to watch them grow and thrive is a delight in itself. Each week there are changes to note and enjoy. Make many and keep some. Give others away as a small part of yourself. Find a jar, choose a plant, pick up a smooth stone and put them together in a way that has never quite been done before. Let your terrariums represent a small part of the creative you captured in a miniature world.

Start right now . . . oh, and by the way, good luck!

INDEX

Clip and Mail This Special Shipping Label and...